The Wealthy Ski Bum

10 Steps to a Successful Retirement

—

Sandro Rossini

Dedication

To those who feel powerless over their financial future.

Contents

Who should read this book

As a youth, I was never much for reading instructions or taking a lesson before I learned something new. My first attempts at skiing, for example, began with me charging down an advanced run, in Levi's jeans and a T-shirt, completely out of control. I spent more time tumbling down the mountain than I did skiing. My wife, on the other hand, likes to research everything before doing anything new. But even for those detailed researchers, a multilayered and potentially stressful topic like personal finance can be overwhelming and confusing. Barreling through it isn't a smart option either. It's hard to know where to begin or who to trust for advice. The unfortunate result is avoidance of the topic altogether and inaction. No plan at all. And the years roll on.

Too many people either freeze or dive in headlong when faced with planning something that's 10, 20, or 30 years out—like retirement. I get it. It's hard to think that far out when scheduling even tomorrow is a challenge. If you've done nothing to plan for retirement, this book is for you. Whether you're 20 or 50, you owe it to yourself to have a solid plan and to understand what it will take to retire—even if you don't love all of the steps to get there. Or if you've already made a move and are regularly putting money into a retirement account but have no idea what you're doing, this book can also help.

And if you have turned to the professionals for advice about your retirement account and your personal finances overall, this book is for you too. I spent the majority of my professional life advising people about their finances. Throughout the years, though, I observed the business of providing personal financial advice shift more and more toward the very wealthy, with banks, brokerage firms, insurance companies, and even small independent advisors all going "up market" and leaving middle-class Americans to fend for themselves. In other words, if you don't have the big bucks, you aren't getting much attention from the professionals. But even if you're fortunate enough to have an advisor, it still makes sense to have an understanding of your retirement account and personal finance. I'm not saying that every advisor is Bernie Madoff—but how do you know whether the advice you're receiving is good if you don't know anything about the topic?

One day I received a call from my sister, a schoolteacher. She needed advice about her retirement account and had lost faith in her "advisor." After 15 disciplined years of adding money to her account, she had no clue what her investments were, how they were doing, or whether she was on track. Unfortunately, this is all too common. Upon reviewing her statement, I was appalled. She, and her advisor, had chosen the most ill-suited investments and as a result lost out on tens of thousands of dollars in growth over the years. My sister's advisor hadn't bothered to educate her on the appropriate amount to contribute to her account and how to properly invest. It turns out, the advisor was in a call center servicing hundreds of "clients" and apparently had neither the time nor the interest to get to know my sister and what was best for her.

> **This may be the largest sum of money you'll ever possess. Treat it with the respect it deserves.**

I'm not saying that everyone needs to learn how to fix their own car, fill their own cavities, and perform their own medical procedures, but when you consider that a retirement account can take perhaps 20 years to build and that it has to provide you and your family with income for the rest of your non-working life, shouldn't you know what and how you're doing? This may be the largest sum of money you'll ever possess. Treat it with the respect it deserves.

And then there are those who abhor the concept of retirement and never want to go there. Maybe it raises fears of irrelevance or slowing down too much. I understand that concern, but if this is you, the problem isn't with retirement, it's with how you define it. I'm retired, but I don't spend my days lounging in my pajamas. Retirement doesn't equal not working or no ambition. Rather, it's about not having to work for money anymore. It's about choosing what you do every day without money being the main motivator. Having a good retirement plan in place means that you're in good shape financially. You won't have to worry about surviving the next downsizing at work, or a crushing medical bill, or rent increases driving you out on the street. Those are things no one should have to worry about, especially when you get old (yes, that time is coming whether you like it or not).

For this book, I chose to approach the topic of retirement planning with my sister in mind. I knew that the typical jargon-loaded, data-driven finance guidebooks had always turned her off. Then there's Bill, a retired grocery store clerk I happened to meet during a ski trip in the Sierras. His story and our conversation inspired me. He shared his steady approach to building a successful retirement. The everyday language he used to convey financial topics became the basis of this book.

Read this book if:

You have started your first job *and know nothing about retirement accounts, budgeting, investing, and personal finance and you want an easy-to-read guide.*

You have a retirement account *but don't feel confident in your knowledge of investing and personal finance—and don't know if you're on track.*

You're not new to personal finance *and may even have an advisor—but you find all the jargon used by the professionals confusing and intimidating.*

You don't like the topic *and tend to zone out when you should be paying attention.*

Preface

Three-quarters of American families say they live paycheck to paycheck. One-third report having saved nothing toward retirement and being under financial stress, and two out of three Americans are financially illiterate.[1] Among employed Americans, the median savings for those age 50 to 55 is only $8,000, and for those 56 to 61 it's only $17,000[2]—far less than needed to sustain them through their golden years.

And if you're thinking there is plenty of time to begin saving tomorrow, consider this: The landscape for jobs is changing rapidly. Every year, companies are choosing to move their factories and hire employees outside of the United States. The Economic Policy Institute estimates that the US lost 3.2 million manufacturing jobs between 2001 and 2013.[3] Companies that made computer and electronic parts, textiles and apparel, and furniture were hit the hardest. And for those people lucky enough to keep their jobs, many will earn less because of global competition for workers and new technology.

Then there's the coronavirus. It may take years to fully know the impact of this pandemic. Tens of millions of Americans have filed for unemployment, with more to come. Sure, people will gradually go back to work, but the impact of this and the threat of future pandemics may affect our economy and job security for a very long time.

So when you make the decision to save for your future, how do you do it? Chances are you didn't learn how to save and invest while in school (schools don't teach personal finance). What about turning to the pros? The large, reputable investment companies will pass on anyone who doesn't have a big chunk of money to invest. What about an informed colleague or a family member? You might glean some tidbits, but you can't monopolize their time. There are commissioned-based advisors, but it's their business to sell a product and not merely, well, advise you. It's no surprise that the wealth gap is widening between the rich and everyone else. As of 2016, the top 1% held 38.6% of the nation's wealth, and the bottom 90% held only 23%.[4] This disparity is increasing. Now more than ever it's imperative that the average American take charge of their own financial future.

The good news is that anyone can achieve financial freedom on any income level with 10 very simple steps. You don't need to be Bill Gates to have less financial worry, have enough money to retire, and live the life of your dreams.

10 Steps to a Successful Retirement

1. Learn investment basics
2. Reduce debt and expenses
3. Build a cash cushion
4. Create a retirement plan
5. Protect your investments from taxes
6. Select "weatherproof" investments
7. Buy real estate and collect rent
8. Protect your family with insurance
9. Use apps and dreams to stay on track
10. Set up an estate plan

Introduction

The snow fell lightly as I approached the mountain lodge. I released my skis from my boots and clipped them together, then sunk them into the deep snow. I opened the door to the lodge, took off my helmet and gloves, unzipped my jacket, and let the heat from the corner pot-belly stove warm my face and hands. A couple dozen skiers were basking in après-ski mode. As I shook off the snow, smiling faces glanced over. There's always a look you get when you enter a ski lodge like, yeah, can you believe we get to do this?

I squeezed myself into an empty seat at the bar, between a blond woman and an affable-looking guy in his early sixties. As I scanned the menu, the gentleman next to me offered up: "The sausages are pretty good." He introduced himself as Bill.

I was glad to have someone to talk to after having skied by myself all day. We exchanged some pleasantries, and I learned that it was Bill's first day of retirement. A cause for celebration for sure—and I offered a round on me. Bill's plan? To spend the next week skiing in the California Sierras, and then heading to Aspen, Colorado, for more free time on the slopes. Bill had mapped out his winter, making it his goal to ski in seven of the top resorts across the country. Europe's prized mountains would be next. I immediately assumed (perhaps because I live an hour from Silicon Valley) that Bill was one of those tech millionaires—someone who had come up with a new technology and sold it to Apple or Microsoft and made billions. How else could he retire and still afford so much expensive leisure? I asked him, "What was your line of work?" Bill's answer surprised me. "I worked in a grocery store for 30 years, first bagging groceries and then stocking shelves," he said. Bill smiled as curiosity filled my face, and he proudly explained that although his salary was never large, he'd committed to saving money and managing it wisely so that he would never be unprepared for the worst and could quit working sooner rather than later. Now he could fill his time doing what he loved, like going skiing.

Hearing a story like Bill's always makes me feel good. When I was a kid, my favorite movies were the ones about people who had started with nothing but through hard work and determination had achieved their dreams. Think *Rocky, Vision Quest, The Secret of My Success.* No, these aren't all Academy Award winners, but they portray a paradigm that all of us can take to heart: With effort, discipline, and the right direction, it's possible to achieve almost any lofty goal.

I also think that I connected with Bill and his story because of my background in finance. I spent 28 years in the financial services industry, first as a banker, then as a financial advisor, and ultimately as the managing director for the California wealth management division at a large national bank, responsible for more than 100 private bankers, financial advisors, trust administrators, investment portfolio managers, and financial planners. Over the span of my career, I worked with people who earned millions each year but remained weighed down by debt and had no savings. I also encountered people like Bill who had amassed million-dollar retirement accounts while working in blue-collar jobs. I learned that regardless of how much money someone earns, it is the daily financial and lifestyle decisions they make that truly drive their degree of financial independence and ability to comfortably retire. Financial independence is less about how much money a person earns and more about how that money is managed.

Over the next couple of hours (and a few beers), Bill shared how his financial decisions allowed him to live his retirement dream on a grocery clerk's wages.

EASIEST

Step 1: Learn Investment Basics

The first thing I wanted to know was how a guy with no college education, no financial background, and no help from a financial advisor learned so much about personal finance. "Bill, no offense, but how did you learn so much about saving and investing?"

Bill smiled. "Yeah, I guess it's kind of unusual for a guy like me," he said. "Well, I was really motivated to have a better life than my parents did. At first, I was over-whelmed with all there is to know about the topic. I thought I had to understand world economics and things like 'monetary policy.' I picked up a bunch of books you'd study as a college finance major. It was another language.

I quickly realized, though, that being a good retirement investor doesn't require doing fancy calculations. It really starts with understanding some basic concepts and definitions. And once you build that foundation of knowledge, the rest is pretty easy to pick up."

I wanted more and asked for an example. Bill responded, "Well, a good place to start is with the concept of compound growth. Once I understood compound growth I was more connected to what needed to happen, and I was determined to keep making contributions, even if it meant forgoing a vacation or a new car, and not touching my money until retirement. Understanding concepts like compound growth changed the way I thought about money.

"Compound growth showed me how money can feed on itself over time. For example, a penny a day doubled for 30 days comes out to more than $10 million. But if a person cashed in the pennies after just 15 days, they'd have roughly $32,000. All the real growth occurs in the last 15 days. That taught me the importance of saving and investing. Also, I knew I couldn't give in to an impulse buy and lose out on those 'last 15 days'—which, in essence, would be my key to a comfortable retirement."

Why it matters

No one cares about your money as much as you do. But you're at risk of making bad decisions about your retirement or being targeted by an unscrupulous advisor if you do not have a basic understanding of how it all works. It doesn't take much to learn those basics. Protect a lifetime of savings with a bit of knowledge.

A good compounding problem

Financial lingo can sound like another language and be intimidating. Don't let it be. And investing? It sounds like something only the rich folks on Wall Street do. Warren Buffett (one of the richest) defines investing as the process of laying out money now to receive more money in the future.[5] You work hard for your money, but can your money work for you? Picture your dollar bills heading off to the office, briefcase in hand, and then returning with a paycheck for you. Cheesy, yes, but it's a perfect way to think about it. We measure success by the interest rate, or return, that you earn—be it 2%, 3%, 8%, or more. This return on your investment can tell you a lot about the risk you'll be taking with your money. Read the fine print, but generally: the higher the return, the higher the risk. If you put your money in a bank savings account it comes with a guarantee that you'll get your money back (heard of FDIC insurance?). In contrast, if you invest with Uncle Frank—who's mining for gold in the hills of Malibu—there's no guarantee. Perhaps a little dramatic, but you get the point. There are many types of investments with varying degrees of risk. Ultimately, it's best to go with investments that are in demand, allow for you to sell at any time, and have a very long track record. Stocks and bonds and other products that invest in them (like mutual funds) are some of the most popular investment choices.

The concept of compound growth is straightforward, and compounding can be a good friend as you build your path to retirement. Compounding is simply allowing your earnings from your original investment to be reinvested. When this occurs over a long period of time, most of your growth is actually stemming from the previous interest you earned (imagine a snowball collecting snow as it rolls down a hill). Remember Bill's penny example? This is powerful stuff. Albert Einstein, the world's most famous mathematician, called compound interest "the eighth wonder of the world. He who understands it, earns it; he who doesn't, pays it."[6]

The sooner you begin saving and investing, the more you'll have in retirement—though it's not until you get closer to retiring that you'll see your earnings go into overdrive, because all the real compounding growth occurs in the final years. Imagine the shape of a hockey stick: The handle is long and relatively flat, but then the tip curves up dramatically, just like the balance in your retirement account.

A Tale of Two Retirement Accounts

Meet John and Shelly: At age 20, John opened a retirement account and put $3,000 into it every year for 10 years for a total of $30,000. Shelly also opened a retirement account—later though, starting at age 30—and, contributed $3,000 each year, but she continued until age 65 for a total of $108,000. Assuming both earned 8% on their investments, who ended up with more money? At age 65, John had a retirement balance of $749,489 while Shelly had $606,211. Now you might be wondering how that's possible. John invested only $30,000, and Shelly invested $108,000—but

John ended up with $143,278 more? Here's why: John may have stopped contributing, but he started 10 years earlier than Shelly. He earned more interest for those first 10 years and more interest on his reinvested interest (aka compounding). The lesson? Start contributing to your retirement account as soon as you can!

Age	John invested	Balance (earns 8%)	Shelly invested	Balance (earns 8%)
20	$3,000	$3,240		$0
21	$3,000	$6,739		$0
22	$3,000	$10,518		$0
23	$3,000	$14,600		$0
24	$3,000	$19,008		$0
25	$3,000	$23,768		$0
26	$3,000	$28,910		$0
27	$3,000	$34,463		$0
28	$3,000	$40,460		$0
29	$3,000	$46,936		$0
30		$50,691	$3,000	$3,240
31		$54,,747	$3,000	$6,739
32		$59,126	$3,000	$10,518
33		$63,857	$3,000	$14,600
34		$68,895	$3,000	$19,008
35		$74,482	$3,000	$23,768
36		$80,441	$3,000	$28,910
37		$86,876	$3,000	$34,463
38		$93,826	$3,000	$40,460
39		$101,332	$3,000	$46,936
40		$109,439	$3,000	$53,931
41-59		$118,194-$472,306	$3,000 x 19 yrs. = $57,000	$61,486-$367,038
60		$510,090	$3,000	$399,641
61		$550,897	$3,000	$434,852
62		$594,969	$3,000	$472,880
63		$642,566	$3,000	$513,950
64		$693,972	$3,000	$558,306
65		$749,489	$3,000	$606,211
Total	$30,000	$749,489	$108,000	$606,211

Now most Americans don't rush out right after high school and start contributing to their retirement accounts at 20 years old, let alone at 30. That doesn't mean you can't have a successful retirement. You just need to earn a larger return on your investments, contribute more, and/or spend less during retirement. But since you can't predict exactly what your investment return will be (remember, many investments don't offer a fixed guaranteed rate), you should assume lower returns. Better safe than sorry, as the adage goes. You also don't want to plan on living lean during retirement. You'll want to enjoy yourself. So focus on the amount you're putting toward your retirement and start immediately.

Here's another way to look at compound growth and the relationship between how long you need to invest and the amount you invest each month. Everyone wants to be a millionaire, right? How do you amass $1 million for your retirement? Assuming a rate of return of 8%, you would have to contribute $190 per month starting at age 20 to have $1 million by age 65. If you didn't begin saving until age 50, you'd need to save $2,890 per month—a big jump.

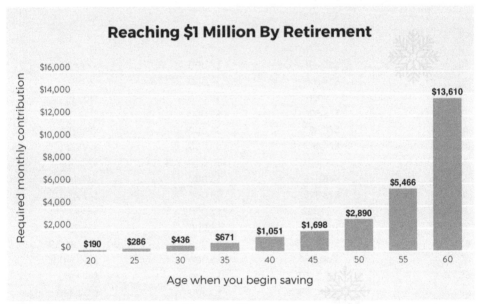

Assuming an 8% rate of return and retiring at age 65

Risky business

How do you define risk? Is it losing all your money? Is it losing some of your money? What about losing the purchasing power of your money? That's right. Let's say you shove your money under your mattress for 20 years. What used to be a small fortune 20 years ago barely buys you a vacation today. It's a risk you likely haven't put much thought into. Your money must grow to keep up with inflation (the increasing price of things). While not as scary as the roulette table, inflation is a real risk that erodes your wealth. Historically, your money must grow 3% per year just to maintain its value. So if your money isn't earning more than inflation, that's a problem.

And the risks go on. What about not having an emergency fund on hand? Or the possibility of losing your job and not being able to put food on the table? Or that you're hit with a medical calamity that makes it difficult or impossible to work? So add to your definition of risk: not saving and growing your money sufficiently.

We face a variety of financial risks throughout our lives, but with knowledge and proper planning many of these can be reduced (I can't say *all* risk can be eliminated).

Now before you run for the hills, understand that risk doesn't mean you're going to lose your money. You can invest with a high degree of success provided you understand your investments, choose what's best for you and your situation, and have an appropriate time frame for investing (short-term investing can be riskier than long-term investing—more on this later).

Since we're focusing on building your retirement account, let's start by understanding the types of investments typically available to you in these accounts.

 Investment smorgasbord

($) Stocks

When a company wants to raise money to expand and, say, build more factories or more retail stores, it often decides to sell some of its company to investors through the sale of company stock (you may have heard the phrase "going public"—as in, we're opening up our company to public ownership). You can become an investor in the company by buying a piece—or share—of the company in the form of its stock. A company will create this opportunity by issuing and selling shares of stock. You can buy a single share or millions of shares of a company. Of course, most people can't afford to buy much of a public company. To give you a sense: As of November 21, 2019, Amazon had about 500 million shares outstanding (which means available for sale).[7] That means if you had bought one share, you would own 0.0000002% of Amazon. But you're not buying Amazon to take it over. You're buying stock in the hope of making money. The price of a company's stock can climb if the earnings and potential for further growth are good. One company that has historically experienced incredible growth is Apple. If you had invested $1,000 in Apple when it went public in 1980, your shares would be worth roughly $8 million today.[8] Definitely not the typical stock experience. For every Apple stock success there are countless company stock failures. Remember Compaq Computers, Radio Shack, Circuit City, Blockbuster, and Enron?

Investing in winners sounds exciting. Investing in losers sucks. So keep a clear head, because you're planning for retirement, not gambling: Stock prices hinge on a company's anticipated performance. Investors are predicting how well a company will perform in the future. Are the company's products or services good? Can the company generate money? And larger and even more complicated influences come into play, like the economy, global competition and demand for products and services, politics, and natural disasters. This is why diversifying your portfolio of stocks is critical and it's best not to plunge a big chunk of money into one type of stock, but rather select many stocks from many sectors, such as finance, industrial, technology, and health care. Consider various sizes of companies in and outside the US. Sticking with just one, two, or even five stocks is too risky. The math speaks for itself: If just one of the five company stocks you own goes under, you will lose 20 percent of your money. You may not have enough money to buy hundreds of stocks—but there is a solution to your problem, and it's called a mutual fund, which I describe later in this chapter.

($) Bonds

Another way a company raises money is through a type of loan—through something called bonds. Just like you'd go to a bank for a personal loan, an auto loan, or a mortgage, a company can turn to a bank. But can you picture General Motors walking into a local bank branch and asking for a loan? When the company feels that the bank's interest rates, fees, or restrictions are too great, it has another option. Instead of borrowing from a bank, it can borrow from you by selling you a bond.

You and other investors can buy a company's bonds (and stock) through Charles Schwab, Fidelity, or other brokerage companies. When you do this, the company agrees to pay you an interest rate for a certain period of time, until the bond reaches "maturity." Not only can a company issue and sell its bonds, but so can the federal government. Government bonds, also known as Treasury bonds, are considered the safest type. Why? Because they're guaranteed by the federal government. But this lower risk also equals a lower level of interest. Generally, the lower the risk, the lower the interest rate. The federal government has never failed to pay back on any bond it has issued (and if it were to, you and I would likely have much bigger problems than just getting our money back from our bonds). If you opt to sell your bonds prior to maturity, you may get more or less than what you had paid—depending on what other investors would pay for your bonds. Because bonds offer a guarantee, they are generally considered safer than stocks. (Stocks offer no guarantee.)

($) Mutual funds

There are thousands of mutual funds to choose from, and they fall into two basic categories: Active mutual funds try to pick the best stocks and bonds, and passive mutual funds spread your money across a large number of stocks and bonds and hold them for the long haul. In study after study, the active mutual funds often perform worse than the passive type.[9] But here's the clincher—the active mutual funds also charge more fees than the passive.[10] These fees go to pay the "stock pro" who's trying to select the best stocks to purchase or sell. (You'd think they'd charge less for worse results.)

Like a stock or a bond, a mutual fund can be purchased through a brokerage company; but unlike a stock or a bond, they are offered within your employer's retirement plan, be it a 401(k) or 403(b), or within your SEP if you're self-employed. A mutual fund is an investment account that is professionally managed to a particular goal, like for growth (aggressive) or income (less aggressive). You can invest in a mutual fund through the purchase of shares. Your ownership in these shares entitles you to reap a proportional share of the growth (or loss) of the mutual fund. The benefit to you is that by pooling your money with other investors you have access to hundreds of investments that you likely wouldn't be able to afford on your own. A typical mutual fund invests in stocks as well as bonds, and the manager of the mutual fund decides when to buy or sell a particular stock or bond. For this management you pay a fee. (Some mutual funds also charge a commission, but you likely won't pay this if it's within your 401(k).)

($) Indexes

There are more than 3,700 stocks listed on the major US stock exchanges and about 45,000 stocks listed on all the exchanges globally.[11] Most people may be drawn to a particular segment of stock but can't afford to buy the entire group. So indexes—groupings of stocks with similar characteristics—were developed to track the most sought-after segments of the stock market. Much like how the US Census tracks the population by using a sample of people to represent a larger segment, these indexes take a sample of stocks to track a larger group and report their price movements. The index picks only the most influential stocks in a certain category and throws out the rest. The result: The index attempts to mirror the stock price movement of the larger group of stocks in its category. There are many mutual funds that invest in indexes (yes, you buy shares in the mutual fund, and the mutual fund buys the stock of an index). What's the advantage? You can buy shares of an index mutual fund and spread your money over hundreds of stocks for less money. It's more efficient and less costly.

One of the first indexes created was the Dow Jones Industrial Average (DJIA). Sound familiar? It contains 30 of the largest and most influential companies. However, today the index that is most reflective of the US stock market is the Standard & Poor's 500 Index (S&P 500).

The S&P 500 Index

The S&P 500 represents the 500 largest publicly traded corporations in the US—which makes up about 80% of all US market capitalization. That means, of the 3,700 companies that sell stock in the US,[12] the 500 companies that make up the S&P 500 are 80% of the entire market value.

The S&P only wants really big, established US companies that make a profit. That's why the S&P 500 is considered a good indicator of how the US markets are performing. Members of this prestigious index must, at a minimum, be a US company, have a value of $5.3 billion or more (market capitalization), and have positive reported earnings in the most recent quarter and the past four quarters, and the stock must be easy to buy and sell (there are people willing to buy and sell the stock) and trade at a reasonable price.[13] If you were to try to buy just one share of each of these companies' stock, expect to spend more than $3.6 million—not so achievable by the average investor.[14] But when you buy shares of an S&P 500 mutual fund index you're pooling your money with other investors (kinda like splitting the bill). Many mutual funds allow you to invest with as little as $500.

Top S&P 500 Companies

Here are some of the largest companies in the S&P 500 (as of September 30, 2018) and the various sectors represented by the index.

S&P Index Top 10 Holdings by %		S&P Index Sector Weighting by %	
Apple	4.36	Information Technolgy	20.83
Microsoft	3.60	Healthcare	15.13
Amazon.com	3.14	Financials	13.43
Berkshire Hathway	1.73	Consumer Discretionary	10.00
Facebook	1.59	Communications Services	10.00
JP Morgan	1.54	Industrials	9.65
Johnson & Johnson	1.54	Consumer Staples	6.86
Exxon	1.48	Energy	6.07
Alphabet Inc - Cl C	1.46	Utilities	3.0
Alphabet Inc - Cl A	1.43	Real Estate	2.64
		Materials	2.39

Source: Bloomberg. Index sector weightings and top holdings are subject to change.

So how much has the S&P 500 earned? According to a report by the Associated Press, President Donald Trump inherited $40 million, mostly in real estate, and, according to Bloomberg, is worth $3 billion as of June 2019.[15] If at the time of receiving his inheritance Trump had liquidated his real estate and invested his proceeds into the S&P 500, his inheritance would have grown to more than $13 billion.[16] Sorry, Mr. President. This speaks to the power of the S&P 500 as an investment. The average annual return for the S&P 500 since its inception in 1928 through 2017 is about 10 percent.[17] You might be asking yourself, with returns like that why not put all your money in the S&P 500? Answer: Because those average returns don't tell the entire story. The index doesn't make money every year. Some years it loses money!

Annual Return for the S&P 500

Dec. 31, 2018	-4.38%		Dec. 31, 2002	-22.10%
Dec. 31, 2017	21.83%		Dec. 31, 2001	-11.89%
Dec. 31, 2016	11.96%		Dec. 31, 2000	-9.10%
Dec. 31, 2015	1.38%		Dec. 31, 1999	21.04%
Dec. 31, 2014	13.69%		Dec. 31, 1998	28.58%
Dec. 31, 2013	32.39%		Dec. 31, 1997	33.36%
Dec. 31, 2012	16.00%		Dec. 31, 1996	22.96%
Dec. 31, 2011	2.11%		Dec. 31, 1995	37.58%
Dec. 31, 2010	15.06%		Dec. 31, 1994	1.32%
Dec. 31, 2009	26.46%		Dec. 31, 1993	10.08%
Dec. 31, 2008	-37.00%		Dec. 31, 1992	7.62%
Dec. 31, 2007	5.49%		Dec. 31, 1991	30.47%
Dec. 31, 2006	15.79%		Dec. 31, 1990	-3.10%
Dec. 31, 2005	4.91%		Dec. 31, 1989	31.69%
Dec. 31, 2004	10.88%		Dec. 31, 1988	16.61%
Dec. 31, 2003	28.68%		Dec. 31, 1987	5.25%

Source: YCharts, https://ycharts.com/indicators/sandp_500_total_return_annual

Let's pick a bad stretch of years for the S&P 500. The tragic terrorist attacks on September 11, 2001, hurt the stock market for the next year. As the chart above shows, if you had invested several months after this horrific event, in, say, January 2002, then by the end of December 2002 you would have lost 22 percent—or $2,200 of your $10,000 investment. Holding on, even during tough times, can play to your advantage. Say you held on and stuck to your long-term investment plan for the next 10 years. You would have seen your balance recover and actually grow to $15,432.[18]

It's impossible to predict what the future performance will be for the S&P 500, but experts have studied past performance to understand how the economy, changes in the business cycle, and major calamities can affect the S&P 500 and the stock market in general. To reduce the chance of being hurt during a bad stretch (a so-called bear market), the solution is to invest for long periods. Take the 20-year span from 1996 to 2016, which included not only three bull markets (the opposite of a bear market—good years for investing) and two bear markets, but also a couple of major events, including the US terrorist attacks in 2001 and the financial crisis in 2008. There also were several wars, yet the S&P 500 still managed to generate a return of 8.2%.[19] In the 20-year period from 1987 to 2006, the market suffered a steep crash in October 1987, followed by a severe crash in 2000, but it still managed to return an average of 11.3%.[20] Over long periods, the S&P 500 has been a good choice for a portion of your retirement account.

There are risks with investing in the market for periods of less than five years. Short-term investors should consider different products, like bank-insured certificates of deposits (CDs), fixed annuities, or other guaranteed investment options. The trade-off, of course, is a lower interest rate. The key to good investing is to only invest in the stock market (stocks, mutual funds, and so forth) when you have a long stretch. Over time you'll have more good years than bad, and you'll end up with a nice average return. If you have only a couple of years to invest, you're more likely to hit a bad patch in the market and not have time to recover.

Why the stock market goes up over time

If you plan on trusting your retirement to the stock market, it's fair to ask why the stock market rises. The simplest answer is that it is tied to the earnings of corporations and the assumption that earnings will continue to grow over time. Every year, the largest companies experience improvements in productivity and innovation. Of course, the market can (and will) drop due to economic recessions—but that will be followed by recovery.

Buffett, again, said it best: "American GDP [gross domestic production] per capita is now about $56,000. In real terms—that's a staggering six times the amount in 1930, the year I was born, a leap far beyond the wildest dreams of my parents or their contemporaries. US citizens are not intrinsically more intelligent today, nor do they work harder than did Americans in 1930. Rather, they work far more efficiently and thereby produce far more. This all-powerful trend is certain to continue: America's economic magic remains alive and well."[21]

Buffett's point? Americans create more products and services than they used to. Technological advances are a big driver of improved corporate profit. Think of your own advances in productivity. Bill, for example, can manage his rental properties and investment portfolio from a chairlift while on his smartphone. Small and large companies alike utilize computers and robotics to improve profits.

EASIEST

Step 2: Reduce Debt and Expenses

I was impressed with Bill's ability to learn so much about personal finance, but perhaps most impressive was Bill's ability to stick to his plan year after year. I had encountered plenty of people with financial knowledge, but they didn't have the discipline to save money—so they couldn't invest. To me, this seems like the biggest challenge in building a healthy retirement balance.

"How did you force yourself to save?" I asked Bill. "No offense, but as you mentioned, you didn't make that much money. Wasn't it difficult?"

"Absolutely!" Bill responded. "Especially when my coworkers—who were making the same as I was—were buying new trucks every four or five years while I kept my old Chevy." He sighed. "I wasn't always disciplined. My father got sick and I was on my own, and money was only a means to get what I wanted at the moment. Unfortunately, what I wanted changed rather quickly and I always seemed to have a closet full of new gadgets, skates, skis, and records (I know, I'm a dinosaur) that I didn't use, or need, and little or no money left over. I believed that you earned money to get things you wanted immediately. I was impulsive with my money and wasteful. I was influenced by ads and by what my friends had (and I didn't), and those desires faded away quickly...along with my money."

"That sounds familiar," I said. "How did your thinking about money change?"

Bill continued, "It's okay to treat yourself, to replace things when they're worn out, but it's not okay to spend money recklessly without looking long-term. You don't need to be a miser, but you should stop and ask yourself: Should I spend my money on this, or should I put it in my retirement account for less stress and more freedom and fun later? When I put money toward my retirement plan, I feel like I'm paying myself rather than paying someone else."

Why it matters

A good retirement is not about how much you earn through your job but rather how much you are able to save and invest. High expenses relative to income mixed with snowballing debt will squash retirement account earnings. Understanding these relationships and making small changes to your spending can help set the right course.

Money on the mind

In the 1960s, a Stanford University scientist named Walter Mischel developed a test involving 4-year-olds and marshmallows. Mischel sat each kid alone in a room in front of a table with a marshmallow on it. He told them they could eat one marshmallow right away or wait until he came back and eat two. What would you have done as a kid? And as an adult would you resist grabbing a stack of cash and the temptation to spend it all immediately—or wait and double it?

Years later, researchers checked back to gauge the development of the kids. They found that those who had waited—delayed gratification—went on to greater success in life: higher SAT scores and better physical health, for example. The conclusion: Learning to delay gratification may lead to positive decisions throughout life.[22]

Mischel's marshmallow test is one of the most well-known social science experiments in history. Since then, there have been numerous studies measuring the impact of delayed gratification, many of which concluded that education and wealth had more to do with long-term success than delayed gratification. Mischel was quick to identify one important detail these studies had left out. Some of the subjects in his study were given strategies to help them resist the marshmallow, like closing their eyes, while others were not. Those who were best at deploying the strategies went on to have more success in life. "People can use their wonderful brains to think differently about situations, to reframe them, to reconstrue them, to even reconstrue themselves," Mischel said.[23]

And like in the marshmallow test, you can deploy simple strategies to build a successful retirement, such as reducing small expenses and saving more. The next time you have the urge to upgrade your perfectly functional smartphone, ask yourself what's more important: this purchase or adding to your retirement account to enjoy more peace of mind now and financial freedom when you retire? Simply by asking yourself this question you will reduce your spending and make better financial decisions.

Where Does Your Money Go?

Expense	Average annual cost[24]
Coffee	$2,000
Dining out	$3,000
Clothes	$1,800
Entertainment	$2,913
Utilities	$2,000

Do any of the expenses in the chart apply to you? Could you reduce some combination of these by $150 each month? How about by $250? Assume you're 30 years old and want to retire at 65. You earn a salary of $36,000. You currently contribute 4% of your salary, or $120 per month, to your 401(k). Increasing your contribution to 10%, or $300, will reduce your paycheck in California, for example, by about $250 (depends on income and withholding) because your paycheck is immediately taxed and your retirement contribution is not. Each month, the $300 you put into your retirement account earns compound interest. Could you manage with $250 less cash to spend each month? One less coffee each week, one less lunch each week, or eliminate a cable service? At an investment return of 8%, this monthly savings over the next 35 years would mean an extra $577,000 at retirement. That's probably worth having less coffee or less fast food!

The real cost

What's the *real* value of money? If you make $65,000 per year and live in the high-tax state of California, you give up approximately 24% of your income or $15,600 to federal, state, and FICA (which funds Social Security and Medicare) taxes. That's nearly one-quarter of your income. Let's say you buy a new car. The average cost of a new vehicle is $36,000.[25] To pay for that car (not even factoring in the interest you pay for an auto loan) you have to earn $44,640, or 124%, of the cost of the car.

> $ 44,460 *real cost of car*
>
> \- 8,640 *income tax*
> _____
> $ 36,000[26]

We often forget how taxes impact our take-home pay. For every dollar you spend you have to earn $1.24. That's right. The real price of that car, those shoes, that cup of coffee is one-quarter more than what you thought.

Your purchase	What you pay yearly	True cost (including tax)*
Coffee	$2,000	$2,480
Dining out	$3,000	$3,720
Clothes	$1,800	$3,472
Entertainment	$2,913	$3,612
Utilities	$2,000	$2,480

*For an income level of $65,000 and living in California in 2018.

Of course, your real cost is determined by your tax bracket, which depends on your income. Here's a rough way to calculate what your purchases will *really* cost you: Start with the amount you plan on spending and multiply that times your real cost multiplier. (This cost only looks at your federal tax rate and does not include state taxes.)

Annual wages	Total effective tax rate	Real cost multiplier
$35,000	17%	1.17x
$45,000	19%	1.19x
$55,000	21%	1.21x
$65,000	24%	1.24x
$75,000	26%	1.26x
$85,000	28%	1.28x

Your real cost multiplier goes up as your salary rises because your tax rate goes up. Say you're going to buy a car with a price of $25,000. If you're making $35,000 annually, you'll need to earn $29,250 (before income taxes) to buy that car ($25,000 x 1.17). By comparison, if your salary is $85,000, you have to earn $32,000 before taxes to buy that same car ($25,000 x 1.28).

What's the lesson? The things that you buy cost more than you think. Be wise in what you spend your money on and the price you pay.

Good habits

Our daily spending habits have a huge impact, and we often don't realize where our money goes. You've probably experienced this yourself: The more money you make, the more you spend. The best method for managing your money is to remove some of it from your grasp—namely, deduct it from your paycheck and direct it into your retirement account. Most employers provide this service via a payroll deduction. If your employer doesn't offer this service, or if you're self-employed, the company that manages your retirement plan can deduct an amount from your bank checking account each month. Like the retirement calculators, there are a variety of websites that will help you set up a budget, but the best budgeting process is to total all your fixed recurring expenses (rent or mortgage, auto loan, tuition, food, utilities, entertainment) and make sure you have six months' worth of your monthly expenses in an "emergency reserve" savings account. Then contribute the rest to your retirement. More on this in Step 3.

Don't overthink it. If you set a contribution level that's too high, you can always make a change. Most retirement accounts allow you to increase or decrease your contribution percentage each month (check yours). We all have the means to save and invest more. A good contribution amount is 8% to 10% of your salary. Remember, it's human nature to adapt to your new budget. If the money isn't sitting in your bank account or in your wallet, you're less likely to spend it on frivolous things.

Manage your debt

Debt is the scourge of a good retirement plan. Why? You're socking away a portion of your paycheck with the long-term goal of earning 8% or more, but at the same time you're paying 15% to 20% in credit card interest. It's impossible to grow your money in this way. In 2018, the combined credit card, student loan, auto loan, and personal loan balances for Americans exceeded $4 trillion.[27] While debt can help you purchase life's necessities, it can also undermine your retirement plan if it's not managed properly.

- **List your debt**
  Start with a list of all your debts, who you owe, the balance, the payment due date, minimum payment, and, most important, the interest rate you pay. You can order a free copy of your credit report via a variety of websites (search for "free credit report"). You'll have to go online or call each creditor to get your current balance and interest rate.

- **Understand the true cost of debt**
  To better understand how much your debt is costing you, try using a loan calculator. For example, a $30,000 auto loan at 4.5% interest over five years will cost you $3,557.43 in interest.[28] Credit card debt can be far worse. For example, if you have a credit card balance of $20,000 and are paying the typical rate of 18%, even with a monthly payment of $500 you'll wind up paying $10,772 in interest alone (nearly the amount you borrowed).[29]

- **Make timely payments**
  It's important to at least make your minimum payments each month. Creditors will typically charge a late fee and damage your credit score if you pay late. A damaged credit score can limit your ability to get

credit in the future and, even if credit is available, it can cause the interest rate to be higher. Just like you did for your retirement contributions, try setting up automatic payments from your checking account. Most of the creditors offer this service, and it can reduce the risk of mailing your check late.

- **Reduce debt**
  Making the minimum payments on your high-interest debt doesn't reduce your balances, and you will pay a mountain of interest. Squash the debt faster by making additional payments, even if it means smaller contributions to your retirement plan until your high-interest debt is lower.

MORE
DIFFICULT

$

Step 3: Build a Cash Cushion

"I grew up without any exposure to personal finance," Bill explained. "My mom and dad worked hard, and they saved a little but never seemed to have enough money to handle something unexpected, like a broken-down car or a leaky roof, and they certainly didn't have enough money to retire. When I was 15, my dad got very sick. He maxed out his insurance coverage, and my family was hit with an enormous hospital bill that my parents couldn't pay. We lost everything. I started working at 17, and I helped support my mom and little sister. College was out of the question, and back then that also meant not landing some high-paying job. I had to learn how to be smart with whatever money I earned. My family's experience shaped me. I knew that I never wanted to worry about financial disaster like my parents did. I wanted security. I wanted to know that I could weather unplanned expenses, medical bills, and, well, you name it—but I realized I also wanted more. Time is precious, and I thought, why work every day for the rest of my life? This idea of 'retirement' hit me—something my dad never got to experience."

Why it matters

For your retirement plan to work, you must not withdraw funds until retirement. Having available cash allows you to cover those unplanned expenses without dipping into your retirement savings and derailing your goal.

Cash is king!

Pull together a reserve of about six months' worth of living expenses and have it on hand at all times. Why? Well, not only do pandemics threaten our income but even unexpected expenses could do damage. Cars break down, the tax bill comes in higher than expected, roofs spring leaks, and medical bills aren't always covered by insurance (those lucky enough to have it). You get the idea. These unplanned expenses can wreak havoc on financial goals—unless there's a cash cushion. For reasons I'll explain later, you never want to prematurely withdraw money that you've put in your retirement account. Similarly, paying for these expenses with credit cards and racking up high-interest debt won't help you reach your goal. But if you have money set aside for such emergencies, then you're less likely to derail your investment plan. Protect yourself with some emergency funds and you'll be able to take care of that leaky roof *and* continue investing for your retirement.

Start by making a list of your predictable, recurring monthly expenses. Think about utilities, mortgage or rent, food, clothing, insurance, and even what you expect to spend on regular entertainment. Don't factor in something like new skis. Find the total and multiply by 6. Six months' worth of living expenses is enough to get you through an emergency but not so much that you're eating into what you could be investing. However, if you're lucky enough to have a good deal of cash left over after your expenses each month, use a lower multiple, like 4 or 5. Most people will use 6. For example: If your monthly expenses total $3,000 per month, you should have approximately $18,000 in your emergency fund (6 x $3,000 = $18,000). Open a new bank savings account—without monthly fees—for this money. You should be able to get to this money quickly, without penalties, if you run into an emergency. When you open your account you have an option: a savings account that pays interest or a checking account that doesn't pay you interest. Choose one that pays the highest interest you can earn. Shop around for the best rate. Often, the smaller banks will pay more than the larger banks (they're more eager for your money). Interest rates are currently low, but even 1% interest is $180 per year on $18,000. Hands off this account unless it's an emergency.

If you already have a retirement account but no emergency fund, don't close your retirement account—but turn off your contributions to it and redirect any cash to the emergency fund. After you've built up your cash to about six months of expenses, you can go back to investing in your retirement account. Now the fun begins.

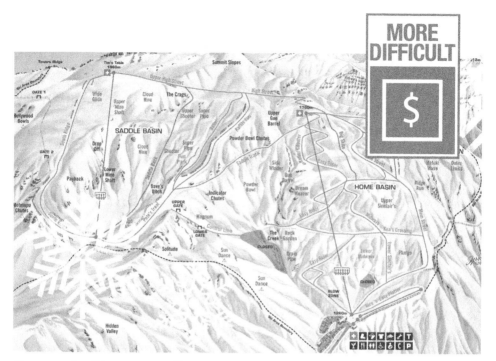

Step 4: Create a Retirement Plan

I asked Bill if he had known where to start. "Absolutely not," he said. "It was both overwhelming and complicated, and a guidebook of sorts would have been great to have. Who knows if I would have retired even earlier? I turned to the only real success I'd had in my life up to that point—running track in high school. We had an excellent coach, and he led us to win the county finals nearly every year. At the beginning of the season, our coach would ask us to set a goal, and then he helped us build a training plan specific to that goal. It worked. It always made me a better runner. I thought maybe that pattern of setting specific goals—and achieving them one by one—would work for my retirement planning. The big goal I set was to retire at age 63, live off investments, and do and have the things I wanted. For me, that meant skiing whenever and wherever I wanted."

I was confused. "How did you know what goal to set? I mean, your retirement was over 40 years away. How did you know how much money you needed to save?"

"Well, back then there was no internet and there certainly weren't free retirement calculators that could tell you how much to save and invest," Bill said. "For that you had to hire a financial planner or learn how to use a financial calculator. I sought out a class at the local community college and learned how to do my own calculations."

I sympathized with Bill—while earning my MBA, I had to learn how to do these calculations. It wasn't easy. "Fortunately," Bill added, "today there are free, easy online retirement calculators available. You just need to know how much to save and invest to reach that personal retirement goal. It all comes down to lifestyle and expenses. Two people can have very different retirement needs and investment goals. The calculators online nowadays can project the income you can expect during retirement, be it 10, 20, or 30 years from now. It tells you when you can hang up that tie or, in my case, work gloves and live off your retirement."

Why it matters

A retirement plan tells you how much you need to save and invest as well as when you can retire and begin taking income. Without it you won't know if you're on track.

Retirement road map

Bill decided he wanted more financial freedom than his parents had. Once he understood investment basics and built up a cash cushion he determined when he wanted to retire and what it would take to make it happen. Goal setting is fundamental to achieving any challenging objective. Fortunately, there are ample free resources online to help. You don't need to be a mathematician to put a basic retirement plan together. Many financial websites offer retirement calculators, which allow you to enter personal information such as your currrent age, desired retirement age, the amount you already have saved, your income, and what percentage of your income you wish to invest toward your goal. The calculator will project the amount of money you'll have at retirement and how long it will last. Play around with these calculators using different scenarios, adjusting your retirement age and contribution percentage. You'll quickly see if retiring at age 35 is realistic! Most calculators will offer a dictionary of terms, so I won't spend much time on them except to say that when it comes to your "rate of return before retirement" use no more than 8%, and for your "rate of return during retirement" use no more than 4%. These phrases refer to what you'll earn through your investments while saving for retirement and what you'll earn while taking money out during your retirement years. These rates are lower than the stock market's historical average, but it makes sense to be conservative in your projections. After all, there's no guaranteed interest rate when investing in the stock market.

Let's start with an example. Joe is 37 and earns $65,000 annually working as a supervisor for a ski manufacturer. He wants to retire at 65. For many years, he's been putting a portion of his pay into his retirement account, which is administered by his company. The total so far: $100,000. Each month, 2% of his salary, or $108, goes into the account, and if he gets his expected annual raise of 2%, that contribution will continue to inch up. On this path, while earning an 8% return on what's in the account, Joe will accumulate a retirement nest egg of $934,989 by the time he turns 65. From that he can take income of just under $100,000 per year.

Joe's Retirement Scenarios

	Current Plan	Scenario 1: increase savings rate	Scenario 2: increase savings rate, lower retirement income
Current age	37	37	37
Age at retirement	65	65	65
Starting annual household income	$65,000	$65,000	$65,000
Annual contribution to retirement savings	2%	8% (bump)	10% (bump)
Current retirement savings	$100,000	$100,000	$100,000
Expected annual income increase	2%	2%	2%
Income required at retirement	90%	90%	75% (spending reduction)
Rate of return before retirement	8%	8%	8%
Rate of return during retirement	4%	4%	4%
Plan balance at retirement	$934,898	$1,343,175	$1,479,267
Annual retirement income	$99,853	$99,853	$83,211
How long will it last?*	Retirement savings runs out at 75	Retirement savings runs out at 79	Retirement savings runs out at 85

*Assumes $0 income from Social Security; sourced: https://www.bankrate.com/calculators/retirement/retirement-plan-calculator.aspx https://www.aarp.org/work/retirement-planning/retirement_calculator.html

Joe had been feeling pretty good about all of this—until he looked at how long his retirement income would last: until age 75. One, he wanted to live beyond age 75, and two, he wanted to live comfortably. So he decided to increase his contribution from 2% of his salary to 8% (see Scenario 1 on the prior page). With some planning and a small change, Joe bumped up his retirement account from $934,898 to $1,343,175. He just added four years to his (retirement) life with that additional $400,000.

During retirement, Joe will have fewer expenses, such as less gas for commuting and not as many lunches out, and his children will be grown and, hopefully, stop asking for money. He predicts he can live off an annual income equal to 90% of his final year's salary. The calculator projects that with a 2% raise each year, Joe will be making $110,000 by that final year of working, when he's 65. Of course, you may be different from Joe and expect to spend as much during retirement as while you were working. It depends on how you plan on living in retirement. (For Bill, those ski passes and Irish coffees could add up!)

Joe was feeling better about his plan but wanted his retirement savings to last beyond age 79. He decided he needed to make some more adjustments (see Scenario 2). He started by bumping up his contribution from 8% of his salary to 10%. He also realized that he might have to cut back on dinners out at his favorite restaurant—but the security of knowing he'd have more money during retirement would be worth it. Then he considered what his income needs would be once he shifted into retirement. He decided that he could live very well on just 75% of his final year's salary, which would be $83,211. Sure, things will cost more by the time he hits retirement, but if things go as planned, Joe will have no debt and lower expenses. Most important, under this second scenario, Joe could see his money last until he turns 85. Of course, he could always spend less to stretch it out.

It's that simple. Play with your assumptions, have some fun. The more clearly you can envision your goal, the more likely you are to make it a reality.

Step 5: Protect Your Investments From Taxes

It was time for another round of beers. I gestured to the bartender. Bill's enthusiasm for personal finance (of all things!) was infectious—no doubt a lot of his enthusiasm also reflected his sense of achievement and his newfound freedom from the day-to-day grind. I wanted to hear more. Sure, I knew these concepts, but Bill had a way of boiling things down to the most important points. In the world of personal finance it's very easy to get distracted with all there is to learn.

"I focused on saving regularly, investing wisely, and sheltering my money from taxes—like three legs of a financial stool," Bill said. "I wanted a way to automate my plan, so that I wouldn't forget to make any of my contributions or delay selecting the type of investment my money should go into—or be tempted to spend that contribution on something else. I found a qualified retirement account that did all those things for me."

This was familiar territory for me. These accounts are "qualified" by the IRS to be used for retirement. Why is the IRS involved? Because the money that you put into them can earn interest without taxes while in the account, and the money that you contribute also reduces your taxable income (tax-deductible). An easy savings. Bill continued, "Not only could I put my money into a qualified account for my retirement to save on taxes every year, but the interest that I earned was also not taxed every year. That meant more compound growth. Think about that—money that would have gone to Uncle Sam stayed in my retirement account earning interest and then earned interest from that interest each year. All of it was sheltered from taxes because I used an account that Uncle Sam qualified for retirement. That's a booster to your balance that could mean well over 50% more money at retirement."

Why it matters

Certain accounts are designated for retirement or education. Using these accounts allows you to get a big break on taxes, which can help your money grow more quickly.

Qualified retirement accounts

To reach his retirement goal, Bill chose to invest in a qualified retirement account. There are a variety of these. The most popular for anyone working for a company is the 401(k), named for the section of the tax code that created it (those IRS folks aren't too creative). If you work for yourself, there are several choices, whether it's a traditional IRA, Roth IRA, or SEP (simplified employee pension plan). All qualified plans have some common rules. Your contribution reduces your taxable income, and any money you earn in the account doesn't get taxed until you withdraw it at retirement.

If you withdraw any money from your plan before age 59½ you'll pay steep penalties. Contributions can be made up until age 70½. At that point you must start taking money out and paying taxes on your withdrawals (a formula dictates how much you are required to withdraw). After all, the IRS needs its tax money at some point. Your company may also have a vesting schedule if it matches your retirement plan contribution. (This applies only to the money that your company matches and not your own contribution.) A typical vesting schedule might give you a fifth of your company-matched money for every year you're with your employer. Call it encouragement to stay with your company—or "golden handcuffs."

Retirement plan perks

Tax advantages

The money you put into your retirement account is not taxed when you make the contribution. That means more money stays with you and earns interest in your retirement account. Let's say you pay 33% in state and federal income taxes. If you earn $1,000, you will send $330 to Uncle Sam. Bye-bye. But if you put that $1,000 in your retirement account, you keep that $330 until its withdrawn. And whatever you earn on that $330 is tax-deferred until you withdraw it. Your money is sheltered from taxes for as long as you keep it in your retirement account. I know what you're thinking: What good is sheltering taxes if I have to pay taxes when I withdraw my money from my retirement account?

Because you're not paying taxes on the interest you earn every year—and you earn interest on the interest itself—your money grows much faster (remember the power of compound interest from Step 1). Compare this with the interest you earn in your bank savings account, which would be taxed every year. Let's say you invest $100,000 at an 8% return over 30 years in a taxable investment (assume a 25% tax rate while working and 15% tax rate when retired). You would end up with $613,405. But if you were to invest that same amount in a tax-deferred retirement account— like a 401(k)—you would have $923,752.[30] That's $310,000 more, simply by allowing your money to grow in a tax-deferred retirement account! Yes, once you begin drawing down on your retirement account you will start paying taxes on what you withdraw (but you'll have more money to pay for the taxes).

Employer match

If you put in $100, some employers will put in $100 too. Or maybe $50. Either way it's awesome. Not only do you get free money, you also reap all the tax advantages listed above. Here's how one typical plan might work: Consider a 50% match up to the first 6%. In this scenario, your employer would place 50 cents into your retirement plan for every dollar you put in. Each year, there is a limit of 6% of your gross salary that the employer will match. So someone who makes $50,000 a year and contributes at least 6%, or $3,000, to their retirement plan will receive a matching contribution from the employer of $1,500 (50% of your $3,000 contribution). If you have a matching program, it would be a shame not to make the necessary contribution to receive the maximum match. Think of it as a bonus—but you have to contribute to get it.

Variety, variety, variety

Often, but not always, your retirement plan is part of a larger company plan, which gives you the benefit of investing like a big fish. That is, you can invest in a variety of mutual funds without large minimum investment requirements, which you would likely have to meet if you were investing on your own. Many people don't realize that there's a qualified retirement account out there for them, such as these below.

401(k)

This is perhaps the most well-known qualified retirement account. Employees of for-profit companies have access to this great tool. Your employer sets up your 401(k) account, which allows you to save and invest for your retirement on a tax-deferred basis. You decide how much money you want deducted from your paycheck and deposited to your account (subject to IRS limits). Your contribution will be a percentage of your salary. But you don't just want some tax perks—you want it to grow, right? That's where you select your investments. The most common investment in a 401(k) is in mutual funds (more on that in Step 6). Once you decide how much to contribute and how to invest, everything is on

> Once you decide how much to contribute and how to invest, everything is on auto-pilot.

auto-pilot: Your company deducts the money from your paycheck and sends it to your 401(k) and invests it. Bill likes this feature because he doesn't have to remember to write a check each month. And don't worry—if you need to make a change you can. It may be possible to change your contribution percentage or selected investments as frequently as monthly (but that would be a bit much).

403(b)

A 403(b) plan, also known as a tax-sheltered annuity plan, is very similar to a 401(k). A 403(b) is a retirement plan for employees of public schools and other tax-exempt organizations—schoolteachers, nurses, and the like. The plan is administered by an insurance company through your employer. Like with a 401(k), you can invest in mutual funds. Another option is a fixed-rate contract with the insurance company, which means you can lock your money into a term, like five, seven, or ten years with a guaranteed interest rate. These rates are generally lower than what you would earn in a mutual fund, but unlike with a mutual fund, your investment would be guaranteed by the insurance company to never lose value (provided the insurance company is still around). I'm not a huge fan of the fixed-rate options, unless you're close to retirement and can't take the risk of mutual funds (more on this in Step 6).

Common plans for the self-employed

For anyone self-employed—think freelance writers, hairstylists, painting contractors, and other small-business owners—there are a variety of options, including a simplified employee pension (SEP), Keogh, or your very own 401(k). The best choice depends on the size of your company, number of employees, cost to set up and administer, and expected participation of your employees (if you have any). You get the same tax benefits as those employees with a 401(k) or 403(b) and have the ability to invest in mutual funds. The most popular plan for self-employed people who have zero to five employees is a SEP IRA (IRA stands for individual retirement account). Accounts can be opened at a brokerage firm (like Fidelity Investments, Charles Schwab, and many others). Contributions are tax-deductible for the business. The upside is pretty good: For example, in 2020 you can contribute 25% of your net earnings, or $57,000, whichever is less.[31] And if you have a bad year, you don't have to contribute to your SEP. But beware: If you have employees you must contribute the same percentage of their salary to their SEP IRA as you do to yours. For example, if you contribute 15% of your compensation you must also make a 15% contribution for each employee. But you can set some minimum standards for your employees to take part in the SEP, such as they:

- have worked for you three out of the past five years.
- have earned more than $600 in the past year (as of 2020).
- are age 21 or older.[32]

It's okay to have less restrictive participation requirements than those listed above, but not more restrictive ones. Bonus: If you're struggling to keep good employees, this could be a great way to retain them.

Traditional IRA and Roth IRA

In general, provided you have a good 401(k) or 403(b) plan at work with low fees, good investment selections, and a company-matching program (free money), look to max out your 401(k) or 403(b) contributions before you consider IRAs. If you're doing that and have paid off all bad debt (think credit cards and high-interest loans), then consider opening a traditional or a Roth IRA. Realize that if you're a high earner you may not reap the full tax benefits of the IRA.

Traditional IRA

A traditional IRA is similar to the other qualified retirement plans discussed here, except it's not offered through an employer, and there are different contribution rules. Your contributions are tax-deductible, like with your 401(k), as long as you or your spouse do not contribute to a 401(k) at work (or to another qualified retirement plan). If you participate in a 401(k) plan and earn a modified adjusted gross income greater than a certain amount, which is set by Congress, you start to lose your ability to deduct. (In 2020, that number was $64,000 as a single tax filer, or more than $104,000 as married joint filers.[33]) Come on, you didn't think the IRS would let you squirrel away all your money without paying some taxes?

Roth IRA

Unlike with traditional IRAs, the contributions that you make to your Roth IRA are not tax-deductible, but the good news is that you never have to pay taxes on the interest you earn, unless you withdraw before age 59½. As you recall, upon retirement most of your balance will have been created by the growth you earned on your investment. That's right, all that growth is tax-free. And withdrawals are never required. A Roth sounds pretty good. What's the catch? There are restrictions for high earners, namely "phasing out"—the more you earn, the less you can contribute to it each year, and if you earn over $139,000 (as an individual tax filer or $206,000 as a married couple in 2020), you can't contribute to a Roth. Everyone else should consider investing in a Roth IRA.[34]

Summary: Traditional IRA vs. Roth IRA

- The tax advantage of a traditional IRA is that your contributions are tax-deductible.

- The tax advantage of a Roth IRA is that your withdrawals in retirement are not taxed.

2020 IRA Limits[35]

Roth and traditional IRA contribution limit	$6,000 per person
Roth and traditional IRA contribution limit if 50 or older	$7,000 per person
Roth IRA income limits (single filers)	Phaseout starts at $124,000, ineligible at $139,000
Roth IRA income limits (married filing jointly)	Phaseout starts at $196,000, ineligible at $206,000

Caution: Penalties for early withdrawal!

Of course, there are always some strings attached. A 401(k), 403(b), SEP, Roth IRA, and traditional IRA are all considered retirement accounts, which means you're not using them to buy a new car next year. You are required to leave the money in your retirement-qualified account until age 59½. If you withdraw any money prior to 59½, you will pay a whopping 10% federal tax penalty as well as a state penalty (varies by state) and regular income taxes on what you withdraw (remember, your money was never taxed when you earned it—but it will be when you take it out of the account). In addition, if you have a 403(b), you may have a vesting schedule that charges you a fee, depending on how many years you've been in the plan. There are steep penalties to deter early withdrawals. An alternative to withdrawing and paying penalties is to borrow money from your retirement account. Many plans allow you to take a loan. You have a repayment plan just like you would with a bank except that you pay interest back to yourself into your retirement account. Hopefully, with good planning and cash reserves you will have the funds to handle an unplanned expense without needing a loan (even if it's only to yourself).

Have college-bound kids? Think 529 plans.

It's like a 401(k) that pays for school. As of 2019, four years at a private nonprofit college, including tuition and fees, costs roughly $147,000. The average public four-year out-of-state college costs nearly $90,000.[36] What's that you say—you have four kids? Before you rule out college, consider investing in a 529 plan. Like your retirement account, a 529 is a tax-advantaged savings plan, but it's designed to encourage saving for future education costs and not retirement. These plans are sponsored by states, state agencies, and educational institutions and are named after the Internal Revenue Code that created them, Section 529.

There are two types of 529 plans: prepaid tuition plans and education savings plans. All states sponsor at least one type. In addition, some private colleges and universities sponsor a prepaid tuition plan.

Options for 529 plans

Prepaid tuition plans aren't as popular as education savings plans, but if you're very confident that your child is going to a particular college, it might be worth considering. These plans let you purchase credits at participating colleges and universities (usually public schools and in your state) for future tuition and fees at today's prices. As college costs climb each year, you're locked in at the price you paid in advance. Prepaid tuition plans usually cannot be used to pay for future room and board and do not allow you to prepay for tuition for elementary and secondary schools.

Most prepaid tuition plans are sponsored by states and have residency requirements for the student (you must live in the state of the school). Prepaid plans are not guaranteed by the federal government. Some state governments guarantee the money set aside in the tuition plans they sponsor, but some do not. If your payments aren't guaranteed, you may lose some or all of your money in the plan if its sponsor gets into financial trouble. In addition, if your child later decides they don't want to attend the preselected school, they may, or may not, be able to use the credits at another school (depending on that school's participation in the program).[37] For these reasons I'm not a big fan of these plans.

Education savings plans are more popular than prepaid tuition plans, primarily because of their flexibility. They let you open an investment account to save for future qualified education expenses, like tuition, fees, and room and board. You act as the custodian and control the account (so there's no risk your kid will use the money to buy a new game console).

Withdrawals from these accounts can generally be used at any college or university, including sometimes at non-US colleges and universities. Funds can also be used for tuition at any elementary or secondary school (limited to withdrawals of no more than $10,000 per year per child, subject to change). Unlike prepaid plans, these allow you to select investment portfolios similar to your retirement plan's mutual funds. Invest and grow your money tax-free (even after withdrawn), provided the money is used to pay for qualified education expenses.[38]

What expenses don't qualify for 529 plans?

- Transportation to and from school

- Cell phones (a computer for school is okay)

- Student loan repayment

- Health insurance

- Gym memberships

The nuts and bolts of 529s

Plans from every state
Every state offers its own commission-free 529 plan. While you won't be charged a sales commission, you will have an annual fee (a percentage of the money you invest with them). States have differing rules: Some charge higher fees than others; some allow you to deduct your 529 contribution on your state income taxes, while others do not. Fees, expenses, and tax benefits also will vary by plan and by the state sponsor. But you don't have to invest in your state's plan. You're free to choose another state's plan, if it allows nonresident contributions.

The California plan, for example, is managed by TIIA-CREF, a company whose fees tend to be among the lowest nationwide. California, however, doesn't allow you to deduct your contributions on your state tax returns. Regardless of whether your state allows you to deduct your 529 contribution, the biggest benefit of a 529 is the ability to withdraw earnings without paying taxes as long as you use the money for qualified higher education. All plans give you that benefit, so don't fret too much when choosing a state plan.

Save on costs: DIY
With the aid of online tools and customer support, it's easy for anyone to select and manage their own 529 plan. Start by reviewing the plan's offering circular (the document that gives the plan details) to understand fees and investment options. Then you'll need to pick your investments.

Select your investments
You get to choose from a range of investment portfolios (again, think mutual funds). These portfolios may mimic the popular indexes, like the S&P 500, as well as target-date portfolios (sometimes called age-based portfolios). They automatically increase their bond holdings and decrease their stock holdings the closer you get to your target date. This makes your portfolio gradually more conservative as you near college. This is particularly helpful for 529 plans because if you are using your account to pay for elementary or secondary school tuition, you may have a shorter time horizon for your money to grow. You also may not feel comfortable taking on riskier or more volatile investments if you plan on withdrawing the money soon.

Taxes

Like with a Roth IRA, the earnings generated in a 529 plan are not subject to taxes. In addition, many states also offer tax deductions for contributions (like when your retirement account contribution is deducted from your income to lower your taxes). Some states' plans, like California's, do not offer tax deductions. But don't worry—the big tax benefit is that you never have to pay taxes on your earnings as long as it's used for qualified education.

> For a birthday gift, how about Grandma gives you a 529 check instead of a new sweater?

Each state has its own maximum contribution limit, which in 2020 ranged from $235,000 to $529,000 per child (not usually a problem for most people). Of course, parents, grandparents, or other relatives also can contribute to a child's 529 plan.[39] For a birthday gift, how about Grandma gives you a 529 check instead of a new sweater?

Withdrawals

If you use 529 account withdrawals for qualified education expenses (such as for college or tuition for elementary or secondary schools), there's no income tax on the earnings or on what you withdraw. However, if 529 account withdrawals are not used for qualified education expenses, you will pay state and federal income taxes and an additional 10% federal tax penalty on earnings.[40]

Financial aid

Investing in a 529 plan will likely impact your child's eligibility to receive need-based financial aid for college. For many families, the larger part of a financial aid package may be in loans. So the more you can save for school, the less debt you or your student may have to incur. The benefits of saving and investing in a 529 plan often outweigh the costs.

More information

Learn more about a particular 529 plan by reading its offering circular. The National Association of State Treasurers created the College Savings Plan Network (https://www.collegesavings.org), which provides links to most 529 plan websites.[41]

Step 6: Select Weatherproof Investments

In the corner of the bar, a caption on the TV gave a recap of the day's market: "Stocks plummet on China trade fears." There had been a lot of negative news recently, and the stock market wasn't doing very well. I wondered how Bill was responding.

"Bill, have you ever sold some or all of your mutual funds in your retirement account?" I asked. "The markets can get scary at times."

Bill nodded slightly. "Yeah, but I've tried not to let short-term events influence the long view. Of course I pay attention to what's happening to our economy and to the companies that I invest in, but my investment strategy isn't dependent upon only one or two stocks. I generally buy index mutual funds that own hundreds of stocks—stocks of big, successful companies that sell all sorts of things. Bad headlines can make stock prices drop, but if they're still making money, the prices will eventually go up.

"And, yes, I have plenty of friends who have panicked and sold. Especially right after 9/11," Bill said. "It takes a while to get comfortable with investing.

When you begin and see your money grow—and even double—it's exciting. You start to feel like you should invest even more aggressively to make more money. Then when reality hits and the market drops and you see your balance drop—even cut in half—you panic! You think about all the hours, weeks, months, and years it took to earn that money and 'poof!' it's gone in a second. You have this sense of urgency to immediately sell. Of course, that would be a big mistake. I saw what happened to my friends' retirement accounts when they cashed in back in 2001 and 2002. They lost a third of their balance. What's worse, they never put their money back into the market to make up for their losses. Markets move in cycles. I have to remind myself not to get emotional about any of it—the ups or the downs. I stuck to my investment plan, making adjustments when needed, but I didn't let emotions drive my decisions."

After all my years in the finance industry, I knew the statistics. Time in the market is always a better indicator of success than trying to determine the best time to sell and the best time to buy. Emotional investors always lose. And yet, waiting it out isn't the only factor either. Spreading your money among different types of investments to reduce risk plays a key role as well.

"You're talking about diversifying your investments?" I asked.

Bill pointed at me as if poking an imaginary button. "Absolutely. Here's an analogy I use. I love watching the Winter Olympics. I root for the US ski team. You have alpine, cross-country, ski jumping, Nordic combined, freestyle, and snowboarding. To handle all of this, you need athletes with different training and abilities. You wouldn't ask a world-class alpine racer like Lindsey Vonn to do a McTwist on a half-pipe, and you wouldn't ask snowboarding legend Shaun White to race a slalom course. It'd be foolish to think that one type of athlete could win in every event every time. You diversify your ski team just like you diversify your investments. The core of my 'ski team' is the S&P 500. To that I may add international stocks, small company stocks, and US government bonds."

Why it matters

The right combination of investments will give you the confidence to handle short-term drops in the market and get the growth you need to retire.

🎿 Keep emotions in check

The financial-services research firm Dalbar looked at the 17-year period of 1983 to 2000 and found that while the S&P 500 earned an average of 16.29% per year, the typical stock investor earned a meager 5.32% for the same period. That's a 9% difference.[42] Most people who decide to invest don't make nearly as much as the market produces. Why is that? Emotions. Yes, emotions and investing don't mix. Most people put money in the market when it goes up and yank money out when it goes down.[43]

Why would people make such poor investment decisions? You've probably heard the saying that the stock market is ruled by fear and greed. When the market is rising and the media is reporting on the fabulous money being made by stock investors, people want to participate—so they buy. But when those same people see cracks in the market, they become fearful of losing all their money—so they sell and hesitate to come back. They never reap the benefits when the market goes back up. These types of reactive decisions produce poor investment results. Leaving your money invested for the long-term in a mixture of stocks via mutual funds that suit your particular retirement goal has been shown to make more money than trying to pick the perfect time to sell or the perfect time to buy. Committing to a long-term plan will protect you from letting emotions chase you away from the market (or trying to do too much). Once you've

> **Committing to a long-term plan will protect you from letting emotions chase you away from the market.**

selected your age for retirement and the percentage of your salary to contribute, it's time determine how to invest.

🎿 Diversify your investment selections

Nothing worthwhile is ever achieved without some degree of risk, and that includes investing. As a good investor, take an appropriate amount of risk for your time frame and harness techniques like diversification to reduce risk. That starts with never putting all your eggs in one basket. In Step 1, I described investing in well-rounded indexes like the S&P 500 through the use of an S&P 500 mutual fund. This spreads your money across the largest 500 companies in the US—in an array of fields, from industrial to health care to technology and finance. By investing in the S&P 500, you are not dependent upon one company but rather hundreds. If several companies were to go bankrupt, or have other financial difficulties, the negative impact on your retirement account wouldn't be as severe as if you'd put all your money into a single company and it went under.

Even better, you are not limited to investing in only one type of mutual fund. It's also wise to consider the stocks of foreign companies through international indexes like the MSCI ACWI Index (Morgan Stanley Capital International's All Country World Index). Just as the S&P 500 represents the largest companies in the US, the MSCI ACWI represents the stocks of the largest companies around the globe (approximately 2,800 large and midsize companies).

Warren Buffett, considered one of the best investors, is a big proponent of using the S&P 500 and other indexes for retirement accounts. "Consistently buy an S&P 500 low-cost index fund," Buffett said. "I think it's the thing that makes the most sense practically all of the time. … The trick is not to pick the right company. The trick is to essentially buy all the big companies through the S&P 500 and to do it consistently and to do it in a very, very low-cost way."[44]

Asset allocation what?

Before deciding exactly how to divvy up your money in your retirement account, you should know about a technique called asset allocation. Put simply, asset allocation is dividing your money among categories of investment assets, like stocks, bonds, and short-term investments (or cash) and making changes when appropriate.

What's so special about this idea is what it can do to maximize your investment return and reduce the risk of losses in your retirement account.

> # Asset allocation can maximize your investment return and reduce the risk of losses in your retirement account.

Economist Harry Markowitz is considered the father of asset allocation. Markowitz measured the returns (or interest rate) of each of these investment assets as well as the risk, or the amount they dropped, during bad markets. Then, like a mad scientist mixing chemicals, he combined these three investment assets and determined the best mixture. He argued that the best combinations of stocks, bonds, and cash were those that made the most money with the least amount of risk. He also showed that the longer you can leave your money invested, the more you should have in volatile assets, like stocks.

It all starts with understanding investor emotions and investor behavior. Bonds tend to reap less than stocks but are also generally less risky (or volatile) than stocks. Stocks, like those in the S&P 500, usually make more money but are more volatile than bonds. So when the market drops, people get scared that their investments will go down in value. Many choose to sell stocks and move their money into more conservative investments like bonds. As a result, the value of bonds rises when the value of stocks falls and vice versa. Because the value of stocks and bonds often move in opposite directions, combining the two in a retirement account can minimize the damage when times are tough (you lose in one asset class but make it up in the other). Cash, or short-term investments, refers to bank saving deposits, bank certificates of deposits (CDs), money market accounts, and Treasury bills. These investments are considered the safest, but they also pay the lowest rate of the three types of investments. If you include cash, along with stocks and bonds, in your retirement account, your risk goes down even further (and so does what you earn in your account). How can anyone make this type of prediction? Well, no one really can, but the past is there for all to see, and as the saying goes, those who fail to remember the past are doomed to repeat it. Long-term studies show how the stock market has reacted during various events. One of the most comprehensive studies covered a nearly 90-year period from 1926 to 2015 and tracked how accounts with different combinations of stocks, bonds, and cash reacted to different conditions.[45] That included four wars, 14 economic recessions,[46] the first moonwalk, a presidential assassination, a presidential scandal, and a variety of other jaw-dropping events.

The chart below illustrates the point with five hypothetical accounts—or portfolios—with different asset allocations: domestic stocks (like the S&P 500), international stocks (like the MSCI AWCI), bonds, and short-term investments (or cash) over this 90-year period.

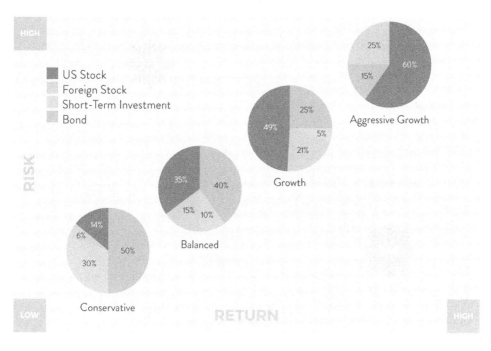

This chart is for illustrative purposes only and does not represent actual or implied performance of any investment option. The purpose of the target asset mixes is to show how target asset mixes may be created with different risk and return characteristics. You should choose your own investments based on your particular objectives and situation.

Here's what happened: The more stock a portfolio had, the more it earned during the good years and the more it lost during the bad years. If you had picked a stock-heavy portfolio, you would have kept your emotions under control and focused not on the highs and lows but rather on the average annual return (or interest rate)—right? On average, the portfolios with more stock earned more (good and bad years combined).

Owning a pure stock portfolio can be like driving a sports car on a bumpy road. You may reach your destination sooner than the next person, but the ride can be rough. It won't appeal to everyone, and some folks will bail en route. Those people may prefer portfolios with a bit less stock and more bonds and short-term investments. The annual return will probably be lower, but there likely won't be large drops in account value when markets are bad. Of course, being too conservative can cost you in achieving your retirement goals.

🎿 Determine the right mix for you

Before you decide which portfolio on the prior page suits you, remember that this is only an illustration and not a list of actual mutual funds that you can buy for your retirement account. Depending upon your retirement plan provider, you may have mutual funds available to you that are called asset allocation funds. But even if you don't have those choices, you can create your own asset allocation combination by putting your retirement dollars into a variety of stock, bond, and cash or short-term mutual funds to create the right allocation for you. Each mutual fund comes with a document called a prospectus that describes how it's managed and what it invests in, and details the management fees.

> Understand what it means to have the right balance of stocks, bonds, and cash—and that is determined by your time frame, your goal for growth (the rate of return you want), and your tolerance for risk.

What's most important is that you understand what it means to have the right balance of stocks, bonds, and cash—and that is determined by your time frame, your goal for growth (the rate of return you want), and your tolerance for risk. Again, the more time you have to invest and the more comfortable you are with riding out the bad years when your portfolio drops, the more you should be allocating to stock mutual funds. Why? Because investing in stocks (stock mutual funds) will likely make you more money over time. You just have to expect some losing years. According to the investment research firm Ibbotson, from 1926 to 2016 small capitalized stock (small companies) returned an average of 12.1%, large capitalized stock (large companies) returned an average of 10%, and long-term Treasury bonds yielded 5.5%, while short-term investments, like Treasury bills, yielded 3.4% annually.[47]

If you have 10 or 20 years to invest, begin with large company stocks, like those you would find in an S&P 500 mutual fund. Buffett is such a fan of the S&P 500 that in his 2013 letter to his investors he said: "My advice to the trustee couldn't be more simple: Put 10% of the cash in short-term government bonds and 90% in a very low-cost S&P 500 Index fund [Buffett is referring to the annual fees charged by the mutual fund manager]. I believe the trust's long-term results from this policy will be superior to those attained by most investors—whether pension funds, institutions or individuals—who employ high-fee managers."[48]

Of course, experts argue as to the best recommended allocation. How you divide your retirement investments is a personal decision. Sorry, there's no one right answer. It's best to begin simply, knowing that you can always make adjustments (trim back some investments and add others).

One-stop-shop mutual funds

However, if you want to employ asset allocation for your retirement account and don't want to buy several mutual funds to accomplish it, there is a prepackaged asset allocation mutual fund option that does it for you. These are called target date mutual funds. They will divvy up your money among stocks, bonds, and cash as well as make adjustments as you near your retirement age. For example, if you plan on retiring in 20 years, you might pick a mutual fund with a target date of 2040. Today the fund might hold 75% of its money in the stocks of large US companies, large foreign companies, and small US companies. The remaining 25% might be in US government Treasury bonds and cash. As you get closer to the target year, the fund will gradually reduce its investment in stocks and increase its investment in bonds—lowering the level of risk and volatility.

By 2040, your mixture might be only 10% to 20% in stock with 80% to 90% in bonds and cash.

Buyer beware!

While target date mutual funds have attracted a lot of investors, they are also criticized for having too much money in bonds, which reduces the return that you earn. One such critic is John Bogle, founder of one of the largest mutual fund companies—the Vanguard Group. Bogle argued that because the yields (or interest rate) on bonds are so much lower today than they were in the past it doesn't make sense to hold a high percentage of your retirement account in bonds. "Seventy percent is too much," said Bogle.[49]

The investment gurus are constantly debating the perfect allocation, but no one can predict the future. Don't let the fear of making a mistake delay you from starting. Far more important is to invest for a long period of time, contribute a good percentage of your income regularly, and include a fair amount of the stock of large reputable companies in your retirement account (via mutual funds). Remember, you can always make changes to your allocation and mutual fund selections in your retirement account.

Step 7: Buy Real Estate and Collect Rent

"What about real estate," I asked. "You've got a house along with two rental properties. How did you pull that off?"

Bill started, "I bought my first house in my late thirties. I barely had enough money for the down payment, but I knew I was going to be staying in the area for a long time, and instead of paying rent to someone else I wanted to pay rent to myself."

"That's an interesting way of putting it," I said, "—paying rent to yourself."

"Yeah, it made more sense to use my money to buy myself a home—if I could swing it—than sending rent to someone else. The way I saw it, every month that I made a mortgage payment I got to take a piece of my house back from the bank. It was slow and steady, and sometimes really tight, but I eventually paid off my mortgage. It's a relief when you own your house free and clear—no one can raise the rent on you!"

"That makes sense, if you can afford to buy," I said. "But how did you afford to buy several rental properties?"

Bill responded, "I couldn't afford not to buy. I did the math. For the rent I was paying I could own my own house. I just had to save for that down payment. It took me five years of saving to have enough, but I finally bought a home. I took on a roommate, and after a couple of years, with the rent increases, I found that the rent I collected more than covered my expenses. After a couple of years I was making pretty good rental income. I decided to save that money to buy another house—this time a rental. And after eight more years I was able to purchase my second rental. Today those houses have doubled in value."

"But isn't being a landlord a huge stress, with backed-up toilets and rents to collect?" I asked. "How can you be a ski bum and a landlord at the same time?"

Bill laughed. "Yes, that's true. I've had my share of fixing leaky faucets, but now I have a list of trusted plumbers and handy people, and I call them. It takes me 10 minutes to make a call or send a text. Don't get me wrong—there was a rough patch. But I can tell you that it's a lot better than having a job, and I make more money with real estate. Plus, there are great tax deductions when you own real estate."

Why it matters

Owning your home not only ensures you have a place to live—no threat of crazy rent hikes or fears of eviction—but also presents a great investment opportunity. Lease out a room or even build an in-law unit to collect rent. You may be able to own a house for the same amount of money you're paying your landlord.

Consider buying a home

The rent you pay likely rises every year (see chart on next page). Want to end that cycle? Want to ensure that you will never be forced to move? Want to see the home you live in also be a valuable investment for you?

Then consider buying a house.

What a combination: You use the bank's money through a mortgage, take advantage of tax deductions, own an asset that can increase in value over time, and potentially earn monthly income by collecting rents. Even if buying a home feels impossible right now, it's worth considering. To purchase a single-family house, you typically need 20% of the purchase price as your down payment. Assuming a house costs $250,000, you'll need $50,000, plus an additional 2% to 5% for loan and other fees ($5,000 to $12,500).

However, if you're a first-time home buyer or a veteran, you may qualify for a mortgage that requires only a 10% down payment—or even no down payment. Meet with your local bank lender to learn about your options.

Regardless of which mortgage you get, it may feel daunting to have to come up with a large chunk of change for the down payment and other fees. Review Step 2. Cut out unnecessary expenses and save, save, save. Or if you're fortunate enough to have family with the ability to lend you the money for the down payment, consider asking them. Put a formal payment plan together that demonstrates your ability to pay back the loan. This could be particularly compelling if you're paying nearly the same in rent each month as you would to buy. Read on and find out.

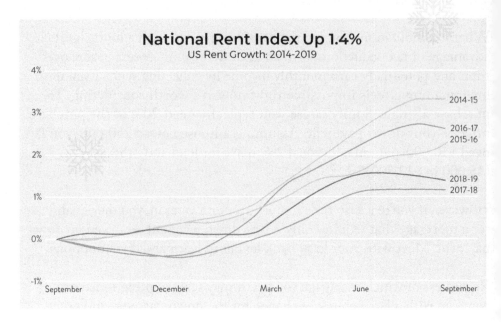

National Rent Index Up 1.4%
US Rent Growth: 2014-2019

Source: https://www.apartmentlist.com/rentonomics/national-rent-data/

Tax benefits of owning a home

You've probably heard about the "tax benefits" of owning a home. It sounds like a special club that only homeowners can join. That's pretty accurate. As a renter, you get no tax benefits. But as a homeowner, you can actually deduct your mortgage interest on your tax returns (for a mortgage on your personal residence up to $750,000). For example, say you purchased a home and took on a $300,000 mortgage. If the mortgage interest you paid to the bank was $12,000 a year, you would be able to deduct that amount on your taxes.[50] Assuming your tax rate is 24%, your mortgage tax deduction will save you roughly $2,880 in taxes each year (24% of $12,000). And what can you do with $2,880 extra every year? That's right, invest in your retirement account (or pay back any borrowed down payment)!

Rent a room in your house

Believe it or not, buying a house can be less expensive than renting. This is because mortgage interest rates are currently at historic lows, which makes your mortgage payment low. If, at the time of this reading, mortgage rates are much higher, don't fret. There's another way to get your payments below the rent that you're paying: Rent out a room in your house. Taking a tenant will earn you monthly income that you can use to invest in your retirement and won't likely require much expense, depending on the layout of your home and where you live.

Now I know what you're thinking—I gave up roommates in college and the last thing I want is some stranger living in my house. Before you dismiss this idea, hear me out. I'm suggesting that you rent short-term versus having a long-term roommate. You can often charge more on a per-night basis than with long-term stays. You're competing with hotels and motels rather than apartments. Your guests are traveling for work, on vacation, or visiting family or friends.

> **Taking a tenant will earn you income that you can invest.**

Companies like Airbnb, Vacation Rentals By Owner, and TripAdvisor make renting on a short-term basis much easier to do than when Bill started renting a room in his house. Airbnb is one of the most popular sites. As of April 2019, the company had more than 6 million rental listings in 191 countries. On any given night, 2 million people are staying in Airbnb rentals around the world.[51]

Airbnb guests are required to follow an established set of rules. They are also rated by their hosts, which allows owners like you to check if there are any past issues. In case of problems, Airbnb provides $1 million in property damage protection and another $1 million in insurance against loss.[52]

Rental rates are often lower than hotels. They also offer more locations. Most hotels are in city centers. That may be fine for those who are going to a work conference but not for many others. If, for example, someone is visiting a friend for the weekend, but the friend doesn't have a spare room, that guest will go to Airbnb and likely find an available room nearby— potentially yours.

Going the short-term-rental route also allows you to have your privacy when you want it. Have a lot going on in a particular month? Block out those dates on your rental advertisement. Live in an area that attracts visitors in the summer but not in the winter? Then don't plan to rent in the winter. You can also bump up your nightly rate during peak rental periods for more profit.

There are no sign-up or membership fees with Airbnb, but the company takes 2% to 3% of your rent, depending upon how long the stay is. Go to Airbnb to assess how much rental income you might generate from renting out a room or renting your entire house.[53] To rent a room in my own house, I could earn approximately $900 per month. Piling that extra $900 toward my retirement account could reap big benefits. At an investment return of 8%, for instance, over five years you would have more than $67,000. In 20 years, you would have more than half a million dollars ($534,552). Pocket the rental income and increase your payroll deduction to your 401(k) by that amount or buy another rental house like Bill did.

Even after factoring in the responsibility of changing the sheets, cleaning the bathroom, and dealing with the occasional annoying guest, the money you will earn makes this a worthy, doable scenario.

Here's how it works
Let's say you live in San Diego and are a renter paying $2,445 each month for a two-bedroom apartment (yes, as of March 2019, this is the average rent in San Diego).[54] Contrast that with the possibility of actually earning money from wherever you live—if you were a homeowner in San Diego, Airbnb predicts that you could make about $1,037 throughout the month by renting a room in your house.[55] Your earnings would depend on how often you have guests, which would depend on your location and whether you accept single-night visitors versus require a three-night minimum.

Provided you could rustle up the 20% down payment, you could buy a $450,000 two-bedroom house in San Diego and pay less each month than if you rented—regardless of whether or not you rented out a room. As of this writing, there are 310 two-bedroom (or bigger) homes listed for $450,000 or less in San Diego.[56] How is it possible to buy a home for less than the cost of renting you say? Because mortgage rates are historically low and, therefore, so are your mortgage payments. The deal gets even sweeter if you throw in some income from renting a room. Let's calculate the monthly cost to purchase a house minus the income you would earn if you were to rent out a room.

Buying a house and renting out a room

Home purchase price	$450,000
Your down payment (20% of purchase price)	-$90,000
Mortgage amount owed	$360,000
You'll pay a mortgage each month (30-year fixed at 4.25%)	-$1,770
You'll pay property taxes and insurance each month	-$362
You'll pay this each month before renting a room	**-$2,132**
Earn money from renting a room (through Airbnb or another platform)	+$1,037
The amount you now pay to own a home each month[57]	**$1,095**

When you were a renter in San Diego you paid $2,445 per month. After buying a house and renting a room you now pay $1,095 per month. That's a savings of $1,350 per month or $16,200 per year. Now what to do with this savings. So much of our future financial success has to do with the small decisions we make. When you find a way to save money or earn more money instead of buying something, put it toward either reducing your debt or increasing your retirement balance. For example, say you invested your monthly house savings in your retirement account and earned an average rate of 8% yearly; you'd have made more than $99,000 in five years—or $795,000 in 20 years. That could have a huge impact on your retirement lifestyle.

Owning your home and locking into a 30-year fixed-rate mortgage (when rates are low) ensures that your payments will never go up and could bring you additional income in the form of rent. You probably couldn't say the same if you were a renter. San Diego rents increased 7.32% in 2019 (year over year as of October 2019), and you can expect your rent to go up over time as well.[58] But the real bonus is that you'll have a house that will likely go up in value. According to the real estate site Zillow, home prices in San Diego appreciated 1.2% in 2019.[59] Like the stock market, there are good and bad years, but generally real estate prices have climbed over time.

Check your own real estate market to see what's for sale. There are a variety of sites available to help. Then find a site with a free mortgage calculator to determine how much you can afford. Next, go to Airbnb and check how much you can charge to rent a room in your new house. When doing your calculations, make sure to include additional expenses like home repairs, utilities, and the possibility that you won't rent your home for as long, or as much, as predicted by Airbnb. It always pays to be conservative in your estimates.

 Build an in-law unit

Perhaps you can't stomach the idea of renting a room in your house. As an alternative, consider either building an in-law unit on your property or buying a house with an existing in-law unit. These are often referred to as "granny units" because many were built for an elderly parent. Today, these spaces are becoming increasingly popular and affordable living arrangements for many renters who don't want to live in a large apartment building or who want to save money on rent.

In-law apartments might be constructed over a garage, in a basement, or entirely separate from the main house, like a backyard cottage. To qualify as an in-law unit it must have a separate entrance along with a kitchen, bathroom, and living space. Renters of these units commonly share laundry rooms (and occasionally living rooms or kitchens). These spaces are often between 300 to 700 square feet.

Many cities are welcoming the construction of in-laws to address the limited housing availability.

Many cities are welcoming the construction of in-laws to address the limited housing availability (check with your local planning department to better understand zoning rules and building requirements, or let your contractor do the legwork). Beyond the obvious issue of having sufficient space to build a unit, you'll need sufficient parking. Building a granny unit is no small task, and construction often costs more than you would expect, so be prepared for a lot of work. In the end, it's worth it. You not only have potentially increased your income through rent but also likely increased the value of your home. Consult with a licensed contractor for a bid on construction.

Whatever you choose to do—whether it's building an in-law unit, renting out a room, or even renting a garage to park a neighbor's classic car—if it allows you to own a home, plus reap tax benefits and build your wealth, it's a worthwhile option to explore.

The mortgage decision

For most Americans, your home is your biggest asset but also your biggest liability. The liability is in the form of a mortgage—the money you borrowed from the bank to buy your home. Just as it's important to see that your investments are paying you a good return and your retirement balance is growing, it's important that the interest rate you're paying on your mortgage is relatively low and that the balance you owe is going down over time. With all the great mortgage sites online, it's easy to keep tabs on current mortgage rates. Check regularly to see how your rate compares.

If you find that current rates are lower than on your mortgage, evaluate whether you should refinance (replace your existing mortgage with a lower rate mortgage). It's not as simple as, oh, that rate is lower than what I'm currently paying. That's where doing a "break-even analysis" comes in. This basic calculation tells you how long it will take to make up for all the closing costs involved with refinancing. When you take out a new mortgage—either to buy a house or to refinance your existing mortgage—you pay bank fees, appraisal fees, title insurance fees, and other fees.

Say your goal in refinancing is to lower your monthly payments. You find that with the "better" rate, your monthly mortgage payment will go down $200—but making that change will cost you $3,000 in fees. To recoup that $3,000 and really start saving will take 15 months: $3,000÷$200=15 months. If you plan to keep your house for more than 15 months, it might make sense to refinance.

What if current rates and payments aren't lower than your mortgage—should you refinance? That depends. If you have a mortgage with an interest rate that adjusts, also called an adjustable-rate mortgage, or ARM, you may like the security of moving to a fixed-rate mortgage even if the rate on your ARM is slightly higher. If you plan to keep your house for a long time, it's better to have a locked-in fixed interest rate versus an ARM that could rise (of course, that depends on whether you think rates are headed up or down—more on that later).

There are a variety of ARMs. Most have a fixed rate period for, say, five, seven, or ten years followed by a rate that can adjust. Rates can adjust annually, every six months, or even every month. All ARMs have an interest rate that adjusts at some point. Will your rate go up or down? It's best to plan for the worst when managing your personal finances so that you're always prepared. ARMs can be great if you don't intend to own your house for a long time. The rates are often lower than with a 30-year fixed-rate mortgage, which keeps your payments lower. To determine which mortgage is best for you, calculate your break-even point with the assumption that rates and payments will likely go up (it always pays to be conservative when making projections).

The rate you pay your bank

It's important to consider where current interest rates are and where they might be heading. Rates change frequently. It might be time to lock in with a fixed-rate mortgage if rates are relatively low and you plan on being in your house for 10-plus years. If, on the other hand, mortgage rates happen to be high, it might make sense to choose an ARM in the hope that rates will drop. Interest rates are the lowest they've been in nearly 50 years!

Historical Interest Rates for 30-Year Fixed-Rate Mortgages
Annual Averages, 1971-2019

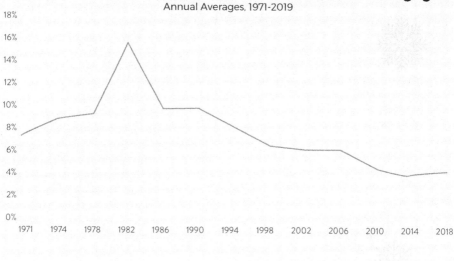

Source: https://www.valuepenguin.com/mortgages/historical-mortgage-rates

Save one-third on your mortgage

Sometimes the smallest change to your routine can have the biggest payoff. Changing how you pay your mortgage can save as much as 30% of the total cost, leading you to pay off your mortgage as much as eight years early.[60] And you can do this without coughing up a dime more than you're currently paying. Instead of making a payment once per month, divide your payments into two and make one every two weeks (a biweekly schedule). When you pay every two weeks, you're making one additional mortgage payment per year (26 half payments=13 full payments). That extra payment goes toward the principal of the loan (that's the original amount you borrowed). By making payments twice per month you're reducing the amount of the loan balance more quickly and reducing the amount of interest charged over the life of the loan. In the early part of a loan much of what you're forking out goes toward the interest and very little goes toward reducing your principal balance (the amount you borrowed). Biweekly payments allow you to tackle the principal at an accelerated pace so that the interest doesn't have a chance to compound— remember Step 1 and compound interest working for you in your investments? It can also work *against* you with your mortgage.

For example, a 30-year mortgage of $300,000 at a rate of 5% means that you pay $1,610 monthly. If you cut those payments in half and make a biweekly mortgage payment of $805, you will save $52,000 in interest payments.[61] Time to buy a new car? No! Consider applying this savings toward your retirement account. Most lenders will convert your mortgage to a biweekly payment plan with a small fee. Check with your mortgage company.

Step 8: Protect Your Family With Insurance

I glanced outside. The wind and snow were pelting the windows. Skiers and boarders were piling into the shelter and warmth of the mountain ski hut.

"Okay, you've described all the steps you've taken to build a pile of money for retirement. But I can't help but think about your dad and his crushing medical bills. I'm sure you've thought about how to protect yourself and what you've worked so hard to build."

"Yes," Bill said, "sadly you can do a great job of building up a nice nest egg only to lose it all to an emergency. Your cash cushion won't protect you if you're hit with a major medical bill. You need good health insurance and, most likely, life insurance. Your work isn't done once you start investing for your retirement. You have to constantly evaluate ways to build and, just as important, to protect your wealth."

Why it matters

If you don't have health insurance, a medical catastrophe could wipe out your assets. Without life insurance, the loved ones who depend on you financially may not have the means to care for themselves when you pass.

Insure your future

Insurance is boring. If you ever want to cut a conversation short, bring up the topic of life insurance and health insurance. Most people associate insurance with death or disability. I prefer to think about insurance as freedom from worry or a gesture of love and concern for your beneficiaries. The good news about understanding insurance is that there isn't much to it.

When considering life insurance the first question you should ask yourself is: Do I need it? The answer depends upon who's benefiting. Life insurance is really about taking care of loved ones when you die. Do you have a family? Are there people who depend on you financially, or do you depend on someone financially? If the answer is no to these questions, you probably don't need life insurance. But if you're the wage earner of the house and your partner, kids, or others would suffer financially if you passed, then get it.

A life insurance policy is a contract between you and your insurance company. You make regular payments to the insurance company, with the company promising to pay out a settlement to your beneficiaries upon your death. There are a variety of life insurance types, but you can boil them down to two basic categories: term insurance and permanent insurance (or whole life).

Term insurance vs. permanent insurance

Permanent insurance doesn't expire, provided that you continue paying the premiums (hence the word "permanent"). These policies also have an investment component. When you pay your monthly insurance premium, part of it goes to pay for the life insurance and part goes into a savings account for you that's called "cash value." You can withdraw from your cash value without paying taxes on the interest you've earned. It sounds good, but here's the problem: Permanent insurance is expensive. There are a lot of fees. In fact, many argue—and I tend to agree—that because of the high cost it's better to choose term insurance. Of course, the best decision

It sounds good, but here's the problem: Permanent insurance is expensive.

depends on several factors, including your health and age. If you're in poor health or older than 60, permanent insurance can be very expensive.

Term insurance is considered pure insurance. That is, there's no investment account or cash value—only insurance. These policies aren't permanent and are commonly offered in terms of 10, 20, or 30 years. Typically, term insurance is far less expensive than permanent life insurance.[62]

Assuming you're relatively young and healthy, it may be most appropriate to choose term insurance over permanent insurance and invest the amount you don't spend on premiums into your retirement account. The trade-off is that with term, your insurance coverage will end at some point. On the other hand, if you choose a long period, say 20 or 30 years, and invest appropriately in your retirement account and elsewhere, the insurance may not be necessary at the end of the term. But beware, procrastinating on purchasing a term insurance policy can cost you. Between ages 60 and 70, term rates can nearly triple.[63]

Long-term-care insurance

Insurance for long-term care provides funds for care in your home, a nursing home, or an assisted-living facility. Unfortunately, long-term care can be expensive, and it's worth exploring whether this insurance is right for you, particularly if you have a family and are concerned about draining your family's inheritance with care expenses.

Health insurance

You may decide not to have life insurance or long-term-care insurance, but health insurance is a must. There's no valid argument against health insurance. The only question is what is the best plan for you. There are essentially two categories of health insurance: managed and fee-for-service. Managed plans have a network of doctors who have agreed to the insurance company's pricing for patient consultations and medical procedures. Users are charged less if they use the network and more when they go to a doctor outside of the network. Fee-for-service plans don't have a network of approved doctors. You can go where you want for your medical care but generally pay more than you would with a managed plan. The best selection really boils down to your desire for flexibility in choosing your doctors or health care providers and cost. Here's a brief summary of several types of plans:

Managed care

- **preferred provider organization (PPO)**
  You can use a network or a non-network doctor, but you pay less if you use doctors in the plan's network. There's an annual deductible (amount you pay) before the insurance covers the medical bills. **Good for**: People who need flexibility in choosing doctors and are willing to pay a bit more in premiums.

- **health maintenance organization (HMO)**
  You use, almost exclusively, the doctors in the HMO's network. The plan won't typically cover out-of-network medical costs (unless it's an emergency). Generally, the deductible is less than those of a PPO. Expect to pay a co-payment fee. **Good for**: Those who want lower premiums and don't mind using the network-only doctors.

- **point of service (POS)**
  This is similar to an HMO in that it asks you to use its network of doctors. Typically, the plan requires you to work with a primary care physician. Your physician can refer you to a specialist out of network. There are usually no policy deductibles. **Good for**: People who are willing to pay higher premiums for more choices of doctors or specialists.

Fee-for-service

Unlike a managed-care plan, a fee-for-service plan allows you to choose any doctor or health care provider you want without many restrictions. These plans usually involve higher deductibles before the insurance company starts paying. Once you've paid your deductible, the insurance company will cover about 80% of the medical bill. **Good for:** Those who want more flexibility in choosing their doctors and realize that higher premiums, more paperwork, and higher deductibles will likely be involved.[64] [65]

Affordable Care Act (Obamacare)

The Affordable Care Act (also known as the ACA or Obamacare) was designed to lower health care costs by creating a marketplace to purchase health insurance. The federal government manages the exchanges in half the country, while the rest of the states run their own exchanges or partner with the federal government to run them. Essentially, if your income is under a certain level, the ACA may provide you with a supplement to reduce your cost. Go to www.healthcare.gov and find your state's plan to see if you qualify for the reduced price. You'll want to select the level of plan you'd like, ranging from the most expensive, Platinum, to the least expensive, Catastrophic. Keep in mind that the ACA was designed to help people who can't afford health coverage. If you make a lot of money you're not likely to get a better price than purchasing your coverage directly from an insurance company.[66]

Step 9: Use Apps—and Dreams—to Stay on Track

I was starting to understand how a guy who didn't make a lot of money and didn't have a finance degree—let alone any college degree—managed to retire with more than enough money to do and have the things that he wanted. Bill embodied the American Dream. One thing still confounded me. Bill spent most of his time skiing and enjoying his hobbies. How did he stay on top of everything: mortgages, retirement account, bank accounts, credit cards, utilities for three houses, rental income?

So I asked: "How do you manage all your affairs from the top of a snowy mountain? It seems to me that the more assets you have, the more time you are bogged down monitoring them. The stock market moves, interest rates on your loans can change, and people can cheat you out of your money."

"You're right," Bill said. "You might think you'd need an assistant or be holed up in an office, but I want to be here in the mountains. It used to be difficult to keep an eye on everything. I had to check my mail for rent checks and bills. But today, everything is available online. You just need to take advantage of it with your smart-phone. I use a personal finance app to track everything—even from a chairlift." Bill typed a username and password into his phone. His screen displayed a summary of all his accounts organized into categories: Cash, Credit Cards, Loans, Investments, and Property. This seemed remarkably organized and straightforward.

Bill smiled. "At the bottom of the screen I get to see how much I'm worth at any given moment. I get a little positive jolt every time I look at it. Tech companies have done a great job of giving us up-to-date, easy-to-read financial data. Plus, they've spent a fortune on making it habit forming."

I knew about the addictive nature of screens. I have two kids, and getting them off their phone or iPad to do homework, eat dinner, or enjoy a sunny day outside is difficult, but I didn't see the connection to personal finance.

"Bill, what do you mean?"

"It's a physiological fact," he said, "that we get a jolt of the feel-good chemical dopamine when we look at our screens. Why not have some of that good feeling when you look at your retirement statement and see that you're on track? I'm not saying that you should sleep next to your investment statement, like you probably do with your smartphone, but instead of glancing at social media five or ten times a day, why not—one of those times—glance at your accounts to see how your investments are growing and how your debts are decreasing?"

That made sense to me. I was constantly checking my screen, be it to scan the news or the weather. Why not leverage our human attraction to the flashing lights of the almighty screen to create and sustain interest in our own retirement and financial security.

But could this enticement last for 10 or 20 years? I thought of my own motivation to complete difficult goals. They were all driven by personal circumstances and dreams. "Bill, is that enough? Don't you need some real inspiration to stay on track for all those years?"

"Absolutely, to stay true to my goal, I tried to focus on the life I wanted to have during retirement—I even covered a wall of my bedroom with magazine clippings from the most beautiful ski resorts in the world. Whenever I struggled to stick to my plan I would look at those images and think about those beautiful locations: St. Moritz, Sölden, Megève, Whistler. It's a great technique to keep your eye on the ball. I drilled it in that every dollar I earned, saved, and grew by investing, would mean another ski turn in the light, fluffy powder of places like Castle Mountain, Alberta."

Why it matters

It's difficult to remain excited about socking away a portion of your income every month for a retirement that's 10 or 30 years away. Checking your progress via an app keeps you motivated, encouraging greater engagement, active learning, and better financial decision-making.

Motivate yourself with a dream

What's your motivation? Why do you want to have money? Is it to care for your family? Send your kids to college? Sail around the world? Move to Hawaii and lounge with a good book every day? Imagine what it is that will keep you focused and gets you excited about forgoing that extra dinner out or driving your old car for another couple of years.

Pick a dream that's personal to you. Then research it, find the cost, think of how it might feel to reach that dream, and set a goal. This is less about numbers and more about emotions. Your dream should get you excited. It should get your blood flowing. If your goal, for example, is to have the leisure to learn to fly-fish, where would you learn? Would you like a cabin near a river? If so, where and how much do you think it will cost upon your retirement? Can you picture waking up early and heading out to your private spot on the river with your rod and a cup of coffee? Would you tie your own flies? Would you have friends who are equally as passionate about fly-fishing? If that scenario doesn't do it for you, that's okay—find what does. When you have a concrete dream that excites you, it's easier to make sacrifices such as reducing expenses and saving.

Technology keeps you on track

Today's personal finance apps allow you to track and view all your financial accounts with one login—your credit cards, bank accounts, mortgages, frequent-flier points, retirement accounts, and nearly anything else that's available to look up online. Many of these apps will notify you if a bill is due or if the interest rate on your credit card has increased. Some will also let you set a spending budget with categories you choose, like entertainment and utilities. At the end of the month, some of these apps will also send you an email charting your progress against your budget.

While most apps are free, they make money through advertisements and offering you product recommendations, like a lower rate credit card or referrals to investment advisors who charge a fee. Some apps are more aggressive than others at soliciting your business, but there's usually no obligation to buy anything.[67]

Mint

Most apps allow you to organize all your account balances in one place with one login, but Mint separates itself from the competition by being one of the best for helping you save and budget. It is owned by Intuit, the folks behind TurboTax. Mint also sends you a text when you are hit with a credit card fee, ATM fee, or interest rate change on your loans. You can then use this information to call the financial institution and possibly get your fees reversed.[68]

Regardless of what app you use, you'll want it to capture all of your accounts in one easy-to-view location, starting with a dashboard (summary) of your balances and the amount you owe. You should also be able to drill down and view all your transactions when needed.

Be wary of those apps pushing aggressively to sell you something. That doesn't necessarily make their recommendations bad, but when there's a profit motive have your antennae up.

Mint and other apps won't eliminate the need to log in to your bank and other accounts for more details, but it will alert you of any activity or changes to your account that you need to be aware of. Ultimately, this will simplify the tracking of your finances.

Step 10: Set Up an Estate Plan

"Bill, we haven't talked about what happens to your money if you become disabled or when you die? I've met a lot of people who thought of every angle to build their wealth but never thought about what happens to it at death."

"Yeah, as much as I like to live in the moment, I know those moments are limited," Bill said *"I worked hard to build my nest egg, and I don't want the government deciding where it should go when I'm gone. That's why I have a will and a trust. When Dad got sick, he wasn't able to make financial decisions or manage his affairs. It's amazing how many people come out of the woodwork looking to take advantage of you when you can't defend yourself. For my part, I spelled out exactly how I want things handled. I don't want anyone fighting over my money when I'm gone. That would spoil the after-party."*

Why it matters

An estate plan ensures your money gets to your beneficiaries and avoids going through probate, where it could be tied up for over a year. It could also reduce taxes for your beneficiaries.

🎿 Planning for your heirs

Estate planning. It might sound like the language of the superrich—something straight out of *Masterpiece* or *Downton Abbey*. Sure, it can be complicated, and setting up an estate plan may require an attorney, but that doesn't mean you can't understand how it works or potentially do it yourself.

Believe it or not, you have an estate. Your car, furniture, checking account, and stamp collection make up an estate. An estate plan is simply a document describing where your money and other property should go upon your death. This should happen in the quickest, least expensive way possible. It should also include instructions detailing who will administer the estate (that is, who will make sure that the money and valuables get to your beneficiaries). It is also important to designate someone to make decisions if you're incapacitated. You worked hard for your money, house, car, and that stamp collection. Upon your death, these things should go to loved ones or charities and not be gobbled up by legal fees, court costs, or swindlers.

Titling your accounts

The first step in estate planning isn't widely known. This involves the titling of your accounts. That includes your bank accounts, brokerage accounts, retirement accounts, and the deed on your house. When you opened your checking account did you do so in your name only or jointly with your spouse?

The answer to that question can determine where your money will go after your death.

Your property can be titled in three basic ways:

- sole ownership

- joint ownership

- title by contract

Sole ownership is, as the title implies, just in your name. You own the account 100%, and there is no transfer of money on death.

Joint ownership with rights of survivorship (JTWROS) means two or more people own the account, and if one dies the survivor gets the loot. Joint ownership without rights of survivorship means two or more people own a specific percentage of the account (as in, I own 80% and you own 20%). This type of account is also referred to as tenants-in-common.

And, finally, **title by contract** accounts have a beneficiary listed (or multiple beneficiaries) upon death. Examples include your life insurance, annuity, and retirement accounts (401(k), IRA, SEP).[69] I know it's a mouthful, but keep reading, it will make sense in a bit.

Probate

Joint ownership with rights of survivorship spells out who gets the property upon your death. Sole ownership and joint ownership without rights of survivorship (aka tenants-in-common) don't specify where the money goes upon death. Figuring that out would mean involving a probate court. It's not quite the Evil Empire, but you want to protect your beneficiaries from going

> It's not quite the Evil Empire, but you want to protect your beneficiaries from going through probate, if at all possible.

through probate, if at all possible. Probate is the process where your state takes over. A probate judge reads your will, if you have one, and determines if it's valid, pays off debts, and distributes your property to your heirs.

That doesn't sound too bad. The problem is that winding through a probate court may take as long as a year. During that time, your spouse, kids, and other beneficiaries don't have access to the money you've left them. And if your estate is large, your beneficiaries will have to pay estate taxes within nine months after your death. There will also be court fees. Many people decide to hire an attorney to navigate the complexities of probate. To add insult to injury, probate is public. Yes, Uncle Frank can show up to probate court and make a claim to some or all of that cash, even if he's not in the will. The judge will have to sort out what's a valid claim. But the good news is there's a way to avoid probate—with a trust (keep reading).

What is community property?

In many states (like California), the law recognizes that both spouses contribute to a marriage in their own way and both have a financial stake in money they earned together, assets they purchased (like houses and cars), and debt (yes, if your spouse takes on a loan, you can be on the hook as well). For example, one spouse may provide for the family financially (the breadwinner), and another may care for the children. So if you buy a house together in California, for example, its value is shared 50:50. That means that even if your will states that your mother is the sole beneficiary, your house will go to your spouse upon your death. (Remember, you bought it together while married.) You might be asking yourself, why do I need a will if I want all my assets to go to my spouse upon death? That's true, but what about assets that you acquired prior to marriage? You may have different plans for those assets. That old car, furniture, and others? A will spells out your intentions.

Where there's a will...

Yes, you can title all your accounts in JTWROS (remember, joint ownership with rights of survivorship) if you have a spouse or life partner. Then all your cash and investments will go to that person. But what about your car, your furniture, and that darn stamp collection? These things don't sit in an account with a title. No, you can't put a label on your couch: "This couch is JTWROS with my wife."

And what if you want your money, or a portion, to go to minors? Minors can't be joint on your checking account or brokerage account. What if one of your beneficiaries is a brother, sister, or friend? Do you really want them on your accounts now, while you're alive? You trust them, but is that prudent?

You can see where I'm going with this. A will is a legal document that spells out your instructions to distribute your money and property that's not held in JTWROS or title by contract (retirement accounts and life insurance). To make sure your wishes are carried out, you'll want to see that your will is written, signed by you and your spouse (if you have one), and signed by a witness. Any adult can be a witness to your signature.

Things can get a bit tense upon the death of a loved one. Without instructions, your beneficiaries may fight over what they believe is their right to their inheritance. A will makes your wishes known. If you have minor children, a will lets you provide for their care. Or if you have children from a prior marriage, a will can clearly identify who gets what assets.

> **Without instructions, your beneficiaries may fight over what they believe is their right to their inheritance.**

You may also be passionate about a charity or other institution, like your university. Your will allows you to leave money to those organizations. Have you ever imagined having a scholarship named after you? There are nonprofit educational organizations that offer academic or needs-based scholarships. Work with them to determine what's possible. Then add them to your will.

Do I avoid probate if I have a will?
That depends. Check your state probate rules. Each state has different parameters for when an estate is required to go through probate. Some require probate based on the size of the estate (not counting property held in JTWROS or title by contract). California requires that estates valued over $150,000 go through probate, whereas Nevada sets the value at $20,000.[70] However, most states will require probate if the will is contested. Remember Uncle Frank? The probate judge must determine if Uncle Frank's claim is valid.

What happens if I don't have a will?
Without a will, your state's probate court will oversee the distribution of your assets. Typically, half of your estate will go to your spouse, and the other half will go to your children. Here's where things can get problematic. To accomplish this, the state will likely sell your home or other assets (how else do you split a house?). This may not be your wish and may not be the wish of your spouse. Also, if your children are minors, the court will appoint a representative to look after their money. All this can be avoided with a will.

How do I set up a will?
Setting up a will is relatively easy. If your estate—the amount of assets you own at death—is large and complex, you may want to work with an attorney, but if your estate is on the smaller side and you're willing to do a little work, there are also a number of DIY websites that can help you and you'll avoid the cost of an attorney. (But before you make up your mind about whether to do it yourself, you may want to decide if you need a trust. It's kind of like deciding what color car you want before you decide on the brand.)

In addition to deciding who gets what, you'll also need to pick someone to make sure your will is put in action upon your death. That is, who gets the money, house, cars, and other assets to the right people or charity. That person is your executor, someone who will see that your wishes are "executed." This can be a family member, a friend, or a professional executor, such as an attorney (for a fee, of course). And what happens if you want to make a change to your will? Very simple. You write a new one or make an amendment.

Living trusts
A living trust, like a will, can provide instructions as to where your assets go at death, but unlike a will, it helps you avoid probate. The reason? A will goes into effect when you die, but a trust goes into effect as soon as you create it (that's why it's called a "living" trust). You put all your assets in the name of your trust—bank accounts, house, and other assets with instructions describing how the proceeds should be distributed to your beneficiaries. Sound a bit strange?

Here's how it works. Jane takes her trust document to the bank and says, "I created a living trust, and I want you to change the title of my bank accounts to the following: 'Jane Smith, Trustee of The Jane Smith Living Trust, dated January 1, 2019.'" Jane is essentially moving her assets out of her name and into a new entity (like a different person). This entity is Jane's trust, but Jane controls it (as the trustee). Jane controls her money and her assets just like she always has. She can write checks, use her ATM card, and make withdrawals. Other assets, like a house and a brokerage account can also be included.

> A will goes into effect when you die, but a trust goes into effect as soon as you create it.

With a trust you're transferring all of your assets out of your name and into this entity. This is so that when you die, you don't have most of your assets in your name—instead they're in the name of your trust. Your estate won't be subject to the painful and public probate process. Other perks? Without probate it's not public information. Uncle Frank won't likely be demanding "his" share of your estate. Also, you can put all kinds of rules in place about when and how your beneficiaries receive their inheritance. Did you see the movie *Brewster's Millions*? Richard Pryor has to spend $30 million in 30 days in order to inherit $300 million. But there's a catch—Brewster's trust stipulates that he's not allowed to tell anyone about the deal. Not quite your estate? Well, what about a stipulation letting elderly Aunt Judy live in your house until she passes away, after which your beneficiaries can do whatever they want with your house?

Is a living trust the best way to go?

Consider a living trust for one of several reasons:
- If your estate is very large, a living trust can provide estate tax savings (speak with an attorney).
- If you would like someone else to accept management responsibility for some or all of your valuables.
- If you have a business and want to ensure it operates smoothly with no interruption of income in the event of your death or disability.
- If you want to protect your assets from your incapacity (if you can't make financial decisions, you can designate a trustee to make decisions on your behalf).
- If you wish to minimize the chance that your will may be contested (remember Uncle Frank?).

Soakin' It Up

The light outside was dimming. It was getting late. I had been talking with Bill for over an hour. The steps Bill laid out for financial security and a great retirement appeared straightforward, and with all of the resources readily available on the internet, couldn't anyone set themselves up for a good retirement without paying an advisor? Sure, but taking those steps is simple and hard all at once. People are busy, and making sacrifices today to reap the benefit many, many years in the future can be tough. But the advantages of taking Bill's advice are clear, and the disadvantages of ignoring them — losing a house due to a single illness, panicking when it's time to pay for your child's tuition, laboring into your sixties and seventies — are also very clear. Not a pretty picture.

"Bill, I'm sure you have friends or family you've tried to teach to save and invest for the future. Have you ever struggled to help them take action?"

Bill chuckled. "If I had a dime for every time I tried to help someone learn about investments, reduce their debt and expenses, or build a cash cushion... I'd be a much wealthier man! On the other hand, some friends have taken to it like a duck to water. I just pointed them in the right direction."

I thought of my own family. I have a sister and a brother. We grew up in the same house. Both are intelligent and hardworking, but they've had no interest in planning for their financial future. Now in their fifties, they're concerned about their ability to retire.

"Why do you think some people take your advice and others don't?" I asked. "In my experience, the people who take action are those who've been able to make a connection between good money management and their dreams," he said. "They have a clear picture of what the money will do for their future. For me, I chose a pretty simple dream—the idea of skiing and having a home in the mountains. Skiing was out of the question for my family when I was a kid. That was this exclusive thing for the rich. I really wanted that adventure. And the key to making my dream a reality was having enough money to retire while I was young and healthy enough to enjoy it.

"It's not enough to tell yourself to create a financial plan and save for retirement. Everyone needs to find their inspiration."

Start!

We've covered a lot. Where do you begin? Review the 10 steps and consider what you've learned. If you have a lot of expensive debt, like high-interest credit card debt, begin paying it down as soon as possible (Step 2). Then work on that cash cushion (Step 3). Carrying bad debt can feel like climbing out of a never-ending hole, but it's the most important step to growing wealth—you can't pay the credit card companies 18% interest and earn 8% in your retirement account and expect to get ahead.

You don't have to understand everything in this book or everything about personal finance before you take action. Think of a good retirement plan as something organic. Your plan may change over time as your life changes. Perhaps your retirement dream has changed from fly-fishing to owning a small island, or your plan for lifelong singlehood was shattered when you met the perfect partner and are now starting a family. Simply go back to your free online calculator and change the amount or income that you require at retirement and adjust your contributions accordingly (Step 4). Don't feel pressure to tackle every aspect of your personal finances at once.

And it's okay if you need help. DIY isn't for everyone. Hiring an advisor might be the spark that gets your plan underway. But remember to actively participate in the decisions about your money. Ask questions and understand what's being recommended. It's your future.

⛷ Have fun!

Having money can change your life. Imagine the stress melting away as your cash cushion for emergencies takes shape. Think of the gratification you'll feel when you own a house that can provide rental income. Sense the relief that will come as your debts disappear and are replaced with an ever-increasing balance of investments. And take comfort in knowing that the people you love most in the world will someday receive the gift of your estate when you pass on. But most of all, imagine all the fun you'll have when you do retire and fulfill your dreams, whatever they are. Look long-term and know that when you leave the rat race you'll have time to spend with friends and family, take up a hobby, travel, learn a language, start a band, write a book, build a business, or even hit the slopes. It's your choice, and it's within your reach!

🎿 You can do this

I began investing when I was 16, after begging my dad to cosign on my brokerage account (I was too young to open my own). My dad had no interest in investing but supported me in wanting to see my money grow. In my twenties, I bought a rental house after persuading my parents to be my investment partners ("thank you, Mom and Dad!"). I cleaned, painted, and repaired that house and rented it for enough money to cover the mortgage and other expenses. When I was 25, I got my general securities license to buy and sell stocks and started working on my MBA. I have always loved personal finance.

But this book is not meant for people like me. My hope is that it will help people who might not have developed a love for or interest in personal finance, like my schoolteacher sister, my copy editor wife, and my artist brother (who'd rather be in front of a canvas than a computer). It is dedicated to those who have felt that money and the management of money isn't something they could handle on their own. To those who haven't been exposed to personal finance in school; to those who have been convinced they must always pay a professional for help with their finances; and to those who believe that they are destined to work all their lives without the possibility of retirement, I say phooey! You can do this. Don't deny yourself what you deserve.

10 Steps to a Successful Retirement

1. Learn investment basics
2. Reduce debt and expenses
3. Build a cash cushion
4. Create a retirement plan
5. Protect your investments from taxes
6. Select "weatherproof" investments
7. Buy real estate and collect rent
8. Protect your family with insurance
9. Use apps and dreams to stay on track
10. Set up an estate plan

Additional Resources

The Wealthy Ski Bum

resource.wealthyskibum.com

Acknowledgments

When I first considered writing this book I began only after gaining the support of my wife, who also happens to be a talented copy editor. Pennie not only made big-picture edits but also worked to weed out the financial jargon. Her push to use everyday language has helped to make this book (I hope) easy to understand and enjoyable to read—even for those who don't enjoy reading about finance.

As I tried to wrap my brain around the idea of self-publishing, I turned to Tad, one of my oldest friends—who also happens to be an online business coach and marketing strategist. He volunteered his patience and skill to design and lay out this book, and take on subsequent online marketing efforts. *Learn more about his programs at **www.tadrobert.com***

And, finally, to Bill. If not for meeting him on that fateful snowy day in the Sierras, there would be no book. Thank you for freely sharing your story and inspiring me. I owe you a beer.

Thank you to Pennie, Tad, and Bill!

Notes

Endnotes

1 Eric McWhinnie, "15 Retirement Statistics That Will Scare the Crap Out of You," October 4, 2018, CheatSheet, https://www.cheatsheet.com/money-career/10-retirement-statistics-will-scare-crap.html/.

2 Ester Bloom, "Here's How Many Americans Have Nothing at All Saved for Retirement," last modified October 24, 2017, CNBC, https://www.cnbc.com/2017/06/13/heres-how-many-americans-have-nothing-at-all-saved-for-retirement.html.

3 Robert E. Scott and Will Kimball, "China Trade, Outsourcing and Jobs," Economic Policy Institute Briefing Paper 385 (December 2014), page 2, https://www.epi.org/files/2014/bp385-china-trade-deficit.pdf.

4 Matt Egan, "Record Inequality: The Top 1% Controls 38.6% of America's Wealth," CNN Business, September 27, 2017, https://money.cnn.com/2017/09/27/news/economy/inequality-record-top-1-percent-wealth/index.html.

5 Chad Langager, "How to Start Investing in Stocks: A Beginner's Guide," Investopedia, November 19, 2019, https://www.investopedia.com/articles/basics/06/invest1000.asp

6 "Why Albert Einstein Loved Compound Interest," RateCity, accessed October 16, 2019, https://www.ratecity.com.au/investment-funds/articles/albert-einstein-loved-compound-interest.

7 Stock price graph for Amazon, *The Wall Street Journal*, accessed November 21, 2019, https://quotes.wsj.com/AMZN.

8 Andy Kiersz, "Apple Just Became the First $1 Trillion U.S. Company—Here's How Much You'd Have Made If You Invested $1,000 Back in the Day," *Business Insider*, August, 2, 2018, https://www.businessinsider.com/apple-stock-price-1-trillion-market-cap-2018-8.

9 "Morningstar's Active/Passive Barometer," Morningstar semiannual report, August 2018, https://www.morningstar.com/content/dam/marketing/shared/pdfs/Research/Active_Passive_Barometer_2018_08.pdf?cid=EMQ_.

10 Pam Krueger, "Active vs. Passive Investing: What's the Difference?," Investopedia, last modified April 15, 2019, https://www.investopedia.com/news/active-vs-passive-investing/.

11 Jason M. Thomas, "Where Have All the Public Companies Gone?," *The Wall Street Journal*, November 16, 2017, https://www.wsj.com/articles/where-have-all-the-public-companies-gone-1510869125.

12 Ibid.

13 Greg McFarlane, "The S&P 500: The Index You Need to Know," Investopedia, June 25, 2019, https://www.investopedia.com/articles/investing/090414/sp-500-index-you-need-know.asp.

14 "How Much Would It Cost to Replicate the S&P 500 Yourself?," Accountable Advisory, accessed February 2019, https://www.accountableadvisory.com/clients/how-much-would-it-cost-to-replicate-the-sp-500-index-yourself/.

15 Shahieen Nasiripour and Caleb Melby, "Trump's Net Worth Rises to $3 Billion Despite Business Setbacks," *Bloomberg*, June 12, 2019, https://www.bloomberg.com/news/articles/2019-06-12/trump-s-net-worth-rises-to-3-billion-despite-business-setbacks.

16 "Trump Would Be Richer If He'd Have Invested in Index Funds," *The Wealth Advisor*, August 20, 2018, https://www.thewealthadvisor.com/article/donald-trump-would-be-richer-if-hed-have-invested-index-funds.

17 J. B. Maverick, "What Is the Average Annual Return for the S&P 500?," Investopedia, May 21, 2019, https://www.investopedia.com/ask/answers/042415/what-average-annual-return-sp-500.asp#ixzz5V3RDU2of.

18 PK, "S&P 500 Periodic Reinvestment Calculator (With Dividends)," Don't Quit Your

Day Job (blog), last modified November 15, 2019, https://dqydj.com/sp-500-dividend-reinvestment-and-periodic-investment-calculator/.

19 Richard Best, "Put $10,000 in the S&P 500 ETF and Wait 20 Years," Investopedia, February 22, 2016, https://www.investopedia.com/articles/personal-finance/022216/put-10000-sp-500-etf-and-wait-20-years.asp.

20 Ibid.

21 Bryan Rich, "Warren Buffett Explains Why Over Time Stocks Go Up," *Forbes*, February 29, 2016, https://www.forbes.com/sites/bryanrich/2016/02/29/warren-buffett-explains-why-over-time-stocks-go-up/#3fbc35513933.

22 "40 Years of Stanford Research Found That People With This One Quality Are More Likely to Succeed," JamesClear.com, accessed October 16, 2019, https://jamesclear.com/delayed-gratification.

23 Julie Carli, "Remembrance for Walter Mischel, Psychologist Who Devised the Marshmallow Test," *NPR*, September 21, 2018, https://www.npr.org/sections/health-shots/2018/09/21/650015068/remembrance-for-walter-mischel-psychologist-who-devised-the-marshmallow-test.

24 Coffee: Zac Cadwalader, "How Much Do You Spend On Coffee Each Year?," *Sprudge*, August 27, 2018, https://sprudge.com/how-much-do-you-spend-on-coffee-each-year-136082.html; dining out: Emmie Martin, "90% of Americans Don't Like to Cook—and It's Costing Them Thousands Each Year," *CNBC*, September 27, 2017, https://www.fool.com/slideshow/heres-what-average-american-spends-these-25-essentials/; clothes: Selena Maranjian, "Here's What the Average American Spends on These 25 Essentials," *The Motley Fool*, December 8, 2019, https://www.fool.com/slideshow/heres-what-average-american-spends-

these-25-essentials/?slide=12; entertainment: "Average American Entertainment Expenditure," CreditLoan.com (blog), February 27, 2019, https://www.creditloan.com/blog/average-american-spends-on-entertainment/; utilities: "Are You Average? Here's What The Typical U.S. Household Spends on Utility Bills Each Year," Rocket HQ, December 30, 2019, https://www.rockethq.com/learn/personal-finances/average-cost-of-utilities.

25 "Average New-Car Prices Up 2 Percent Year-Over-Year for April 2019, According to Kelley Blue Book," PRNewsWire (news release), May 1, 2019, https://www.prnewswire.com/news-releases/average-new-car-prices-up-2-percent-year-over-year-for-april-2019-according-to-kelley-blue-book-300841489.html.

26 "California Income Tax Calculator," SmartAsset, accessed October 16, 2019, https://smartasset.com/taxes/california-tax-calculator.

27 Erin El Issa, "2018 American Household Credit Card Debt Study," NerdWallet (blog post), last modified December 2, 2019, https://www.nerdwallet.com/blog/average-credit-card-debt-household/.

28 "Loan Calculator," Bankrate, accessed October 16, 2019, https://www.bankrate.com/calculators/mortgages/loan-calculator.aspx.

29 "Credit Card Interest Calculator," Financial Mentor, accessed November 21, 2019, https://financialmentor.com/calculator/credit-card-interest-calculator.

30 "Taxable vs Tax Deferred Calculator," AARP, accessed November 10, 2019, https://www.aarp.org/work/retirement-planning/taxable_vs_tax_deferred_calculator/.

31 "How much can I contribute to my self-employed SEP plan if I participate in my employer's SIMPLE IRA plan?," IRS accessed, https://www.irs.gov/retirement-plans/

how-much-can-i-contribute-to-my-self-employed-sep-plan-if-i-participate-in-my-employers-simple-ira-plan.

32 "Who can participate in a SEP or SARSEP plan?," irs.gov, accessed March 6, 2020, https://www.irs.gov/retirement-plans/plan-participant-employee/who-can-participate-in-a-sep-or-sarsep-plan

33 "2020 IRA Contribution and Deduction Limits Effects of Modified AGI on Deductible Contributions If You Are Covered by a Retirement Plan at Work," IRS, accessed March 6, 2020, https://www.irs.gov/retirement-plans/plan-participant-employee/2020-ira-contribution-and-deduction-limits-effect-of-modified-agi-on-deductible-contributions-if-you-are-covered-by-a-retirement-plan-at-work.

34 Jean Folger, "Roth IRA Contribution Rules: A Comprehensive Guide," Investopedia, modified December 12, 2019, https://www.rothira.com/roth-ira-eligibility.

35 "Retirement Topics—IRA Contribution Limits," IRS, accessed May 6, 2020, https://www.irs.gov/retirement-plans/plan-participant-employee/retirement-topics-ira-contribution-limits; "Amount of Roth "Contributions That You Can Make for 2020," IRS, accessed May 6, 2020, https://www.irs.gov/retirement-plans/plan-participant-employee/amount-of-roth-ira-contributions-that-you-can-make-for-2020.

36 Farran Powell and Emma Kerr, "See the Average College Tuition in 2019-2020," U.S. News & World Report, September 9, 2019, https://www.usnews.com/education/best-colleges/paying-for-college/articles/paying-for-college-infographic.

37 "An Introduction to 529 Plans," U.S. Securities and Exchange Commission, May 29, 2018, https://www.sec.gov/reportspubs/investor-publications/investorpubsintro529htm.html.

38 Ibid.

39 Kathryn Flynn, "How Much Can You Contribute to a 529 Plan in 2019?," Savingforcollege.com, February 12, 2019, https://www.savingforcollege.com/article/how-much-can-you-contribute-to-a-529-plan.

40 "Tax Treatment of 529 College Savings Plans," Edvisors, accessed October 16, 2019, https://www.edvisors.com/education-tax-benefits/college-savings/529-college-savings-plans/.

41 "The 529 Movement," College Savings Plan Network, accessed October 16, 2019, https://www.collegesavings.org.

42 Cathy Pareto, "Understanding Investor Behavior," Investopedia, May 17, 2019, `https://www.investopedia.com/articles/05/032905.asp#ixzz5WyOsmlrd.

43 Dana Anspach, "Why Average Investors Earn Below Average Market Returns," The Balance, January 28, 2019, https://www.thebalance.com/why-average-investors-earn-below-average-market-returns-2388519.

44 Trent Gillies, "Warren Buffett Says Index Funds Make the Best Retirement Sense 'Practically All the Time,'" CNBC, May 14, 2017, https://www.cnbc.com/2017/05/12/warren-buffett-says-index-funds-make-the-best-retirement-sense-practically-all-the-time.html.

45 "The guide to diversification," Fidelity, September 30, 2019, http://www.fidelity.com/viewpoints/investing-ideas/guide-to-diversification.

46 "List of Recessions in the United States," Wikipedia, accessed October 16, 2019, https://en.wikipedia.org/wiki/List_of_recessions_in_the_United_States.

47 "Fundamentals for Investors, 2018," Morningstar, accessed October 16, 2019, https://advisor.mp.morningstar.com/resourceDownl

oad?type=publicForms&id=3f9dff3c-f085-47a1-98ba-0bc008df9f25.

48 Mitch Tuchman, "Warren Buffett to Heirs: Put My Estate in Index Funds," *MarketWatch*, March 13, 2014, https://www.marketwatch.com/story/warren-buffett-to-heirs-put-my-estate-in-index-funds-2014-03-13.

49 Rebecca McDowell, "How Do I Calculate Tax Savings on Mortgage Interest?," Zacks Investment Research, last modified December 5, 2018, https://finance.zacks.com/calculate-tax-savings-mortgage-interest-3815.html.

50 Stan Luxenberg, "Bogle: The Problem With Target-Date Funds," WealthManagement.com, June 25, 2013, https://www.wealthmanagement.com/mutual-funds/bogle-problem-target-date-funds.

51 "Airbnb Statistics," iPropertyManagement.com, accessed June 5, 2019 https://ipropertymanagement.com/airbnb-statistics/.

52 "Airbnb's Host Guarantee," Airbnb, accessed June 5, 2019, https://www.airbnb.com/guarantee.

53 "Earn Money as an Airbnb Host," Airbnb, accessed June 5, 2019, https://www.airbnb.com/host/homes.

54 "Rent Trend Data in San Diego, California," Rent Jungle, accessed October 30, 2019, https://www.rentjungle.com/average-rent-in-san-diego-rent-trends/.

55 San Diego, CA, airbnb.com, accessed June 5, 2019, https://www.airbnb.com/host/homes?af=1922719&c=.pi0.pk6440060874 4_285328410852_c_304601193965&gclid= CjOKCQiArqPgBRCRARIsAPwIHoUMultvbG cffybcB_bqivEWj1gDp6bV8cDfSN5ma5YoT-Pe3Gx3ru8AaAiSLEALw_wcB

56 Search for San Diego, California single family homes, accessed June 5, 2019, https://www.zillow.com/homes/for_sale/

San-Diego-CA/fsba,fsbo,new,cmsn_lt/ house,condo,apartment_duplex,townhouse_type/54296_rid/2-_beds/0-450000_price/0-1749_mp/33.197327,-116.62674,32.448361,-117.58667_rect/9_zm/0_mmm/

57 "Current Mortgage and Refinance Rates for October 2019," Bankrate, accessed October 16, 2019, https://www.bankrate.com/mortgage.aspx?type=newmortgage&propertyvalue =375000&loan345600&perc=20&prods=1, 2&fico=740&points=Zero&zipcode=94960& vet=NoMilitaryService&valoan=false&vad=fa lse&fthb=false&propertytype=SingleFamily& propertyuse=PrimaryResidence&cashoutamo unt=0.

58 "Rent Trend Data in San Diego, California," Rent Jungle, accessed October 30, 2019, https://www.rentjungle.com/average-rent-in-san-diego-rent-trends/.

59 "San Diego Home Prices & Values," Zillow, accessed September 30, 2019, http://zillow.com/san-diego-ca/home-values/.

60 "Saving From Bi-Weekly Home Loan Payments," MortgageCalculator.org, accessed October 16, 2019, https://www.mortgage-calculator.org/helpful-advice/bi-weekly-payments.php.

61 Ibid.

62 Kathryn Casna, "Types of Life Insurance," TermLife2Go, November 21, 2019, https://termlife2go.com/types-of-life-insurance-policies/.

63 Barbara Marquand, "When Life Insurance for Seniors Makes Sense," NerdWallet (blog post), August 6, 2015, https://www.nerdwallet.com/blog/insurance/too-old-to-buy-term-life-insurance/.

64 "Types of Health Insurance," QuickQuote Financial, accessed October 16, 2019, https://www.quickquote.com/other-resources/ar-

chives/types-health-insurance/.

65 Susan Niemann, "7 Types of Health Insurance Plans," PeopleKeep (blog post), November 9, 2018, https://www.peoplekeep. com/blog/bid/274219/7-types-of-health- insurance-plans.

66 "Compare Health Insurance Plans in California," ObamaCare-Enroll.org, accessed October 16, 2019, https://obamacare-enroll. org/get-quote/?state=California&gclid=CjOK CQjwqs3rBRCdARIsADe1pfS1WxouSrjeXF- 37pQqX-wQoV6894DaUB8UBmjn_LpjJpIft- VeKt8kQaAjLKEALw_wcB#/b.

67 Brian O'Connell, "9 Best Budget Apps for Personal Finance," TheStreet, last modified December 29, 2019, https://www.thestreet. com/personal-finance/best-budget-ap- ps-14788828.

68 "What Is Mint, and How Does It Work?," Mint, accessed October 16, 2019, https:// www.mint.com/how-mint-works.

69 Julie Garber, "Understanding Owner- ship of Property," The Balance, last modified September 8, 2019, https://www.thebalance. com/how-property-is-titled-dictates-who- inherits-it-3505419.

70 "What Is Probate?" LegalMatch, last modi- fied June 27, 2018, https://www.legalmatch. com/law-library/article/how-probate-works- a-state-comparison.html.

Made in the USA
Coppell, TX
28 July 2021

59618566R00062